FIT
FOR A
DUCHESS

ALSO BY MAVIS BUDD

Dust to Dust
A Prospect of Love

FIT FOR A DUCHESS

MAVIS BUDD

with twelve drawings

by the author

LONDON

J. M. DENT & SONS LTD

First published 1970

© Text and illustrations Mavis Budd 1970

Made in Great Britain by the
Aldine Press, Letchworth, Herts
for J. M. DENT & SONS Ltd
Aldine House · Bedford Street · London

ISBN 0 460 03959 8

The old privy

1

At the far end of the garden path, right in front of the kitchen window, stood our privy.

Obvious, pointed and quite impossible to camouflage, it was there in full view for everyone to see, and I hated it. I hated it so much, I told people it was a summer-house, and when they smiled I burned with shame at being so foolish as to imagine anyone could have been taken in.

Mother was always promising we'd have something better one day.

'One of these grand days . . . when my ship comes home,' she said, vaguely.

Everything depended on that ship in our family. But we might as well have waited for the moon, which at least was there to see. There was no indication that the ship upon which all our future depended existed at all. I despaired that we'd ever have anything better. No one seemed to want it badly enough. Everyone seemed so satisfied and unambitious.

There was a mood of eternity everywhere. Not only about the privy, but about everything else around us . . . in the old, creaking pump, in the paraffin lamps, in the endless dinners of rabbit stew; even in the daily conversation as people discussed the weather and the news and the latest events in the village.

It seemed Grandfather was always saying that the days were beginning to get out, or that they were beginning to draw in. It seemed Aunt Georgie was always in the back kitchen, cutting bread and butter, and Granny always pottering up and down the garden path. And in our cottage there was always lumpy porridge for breakfast . . .

I remember sitting in the sun and thinking it was all everlasting, but knowing that it wasn't, and I wondered what everything would be like in twenty years' time and felt that I was looking ahead to the end of a lifetime. . . .

Suddenly my mother stepped out of the kitchen door and began sharpening the cooking knife on the window-sill. Expertly, the blade skimmed over the stone, her arm in a blur of speed and the steel catching the sunlight.

'Dinner's nearly ready,' she said. 'Five minutes.'

I knew we were having shepherd's pie. And I knew it would be nearly all potato. I wondered how much meat I'd get in my helping, or even if I'd get any at all. The scent of the pie wafted out of the open door and there was a rattle of plates.

The top of the pie was covered with burnt crags of potato, like rocks on some dead landscape.

'I need my barnacles to see the meat,' said Father, but he read the paper as he ate and paid little attention to what he put into his mouth.

I sat thinking, 'We always have burnt dinner, always, always, always . . .'

It was just another of life's eternities.

It was spring and Granny and Grandfather emerged from their cottage next door and went slowly up the garden path, murmuring to each other. Granny, with her half blind eyes blurred in the round lenses of her newest spectacles, felt her way cautiously, tapping her stick against the border stones.

'It be regular warm out in the garden now, bent it Will?' she said.

'Sun's getting a bit of power,' Grandfather replied. He was a few paces ahead, looking for crocuses that had opened since the day before.

'We'll hear the old cuckoo any time now,' he went on. 'She should have been here by now. We generally hears her by April 16th. It's the 20th today, if my diary's anything to go by. She ent usually as late as this.'

Aunt Georgie turned in at the gate with a bundle of sticks.

'Where you bin then, George?' asked Grandfather. 'I never saw you go out.'

'Only a little ways across the common. Getting the morning wood. I've just heard the cuckoo. Over in Butcher's Lands.'

'We never heard her, did us, Will?' said Granny.

'That's no wonder,' Grandfather replied. 'You'd never hear anything, Nell, the way you keep talking.'

Granny said nothing. She never argued with Grandfather. She was used to his accusations. They were part of their marriage and, in any case, were not meant unkindly, so she paid no attention. It was her role to listen, and to take whatever blame there was to take.

Aunt Georgie went indoors and the moment she'd gone, a cuckoo called from the oak beyond the workshop at the top of the garden.

'There she is!' said Grandfather triumphantly. 'Did you hear her then, Nell? Did you hear her calling in that old tree? The spring's here! Cuckoo's come! Summer's on the way!'

They stood side by side and listened for a time, then they pottered on, satisfied, feeling the mood of the new season in the air, in the sound of the bees and in the song of the thrush from the apple tree.

Now that the cuckoo had started, it would go on, beginning at first light and continuing till dusk. Sooner or later the incessant shouting got on everybody's nerves and Grandfather, who had waited so eagerly for it, would get irritable and say that as far as he was concerned it could go back to Africa without a moment's delay.

The sun dipped behind the trees and Granny said she thought she'd be getting back indoors.

Grandfather's garden

'And don't you be long about it, neither, Will,' she advised him. 'The damps be starting to come down and it don't do to be out in the spring damps for long.'

Once the spring had arrived, Grandfather stayed in the

garden as much as he could. As soon as he'd finished breakfast he put on his boots and went out. There was so much to be done all at once. He was full of the plans he'd been making all winter, all sorted in his mind, ready to be put into operation. But once he got out into the open, away from his fireside chair, everything changed. Nothing seemed to work out. The garden dictated its own requirements. The new paths he'd seen so vividly as he sat by the winter fire wouldn't lead in the right directions. There were different flowers blooming in the borders which ran beside them.

He consulted his diary for the lists of seeds he'd wanted and for the notes about new rockeries and garden seats. He went to the woodshed for a spade and garden line and started planning all over again.

Grandfather's garden was small and ordinary, consisting of an oblong plot each side of a dead straight rubble path, which ran from his back door to the workshop at the far end. Nothing could have been more uninspiring, yet he managed to create a whole landscape of mysterious glades and unexpected bowers; the illusion of great space, with the suggestion of long journeys down wide, green paths. He created the impression that there was a way through thick shrubberies to green valleys filled with sunlight and flowers.

He opened a sudden vista simply by the skilful curve of a row of runner beans and the illusion of tropical growth by the accidental mixture of rhubarb and asparagus. A glade developed when he removed an overgrown gooseberry bush, and wherever there was likely to be a patch of steady sunlight, he fixed a seat where he and Granny could sit and enjoy the summer evenings.

He fixed seats continually. There were seats of every kind; for catching the morning sun and for catching the evening sun; some in the shade and others half in sun and half in shade; seats where he could sit and watch the traffic passing in the lane, and seats where he could hide himself in complete privacy. He made them of discarded planks balanced on drain pipes; from slabs of wash-stand marble, from sleepers, slates and coffin boards. He cut the grass beneath the apple trees and there, in the water-green light, he fixed a seat of cord wood. Moss spread over it and it grew into the landscape like an old tree.

Sometimes he levelled a spare patch of ground and laid patterned tiles; oddments decorated with yellow fleur-de-lys which he had salvaged in the days when he had worked in the building trade. With upturned drain pipes as pillars, trailing with lobelia and nasturtiums, he created a miniature patio with echoes of classical grandeur.

But nothing in Grandfather's garden was ever intended to last. He could never be satisfied with the lay-out for long and with every season came new ideas. The changing choice of vegetables inspired changes and the winter dreams brought forth fresh visions. Suddenly, he knew he needed more sunlight . . . more shade . . . a different slope, a wider path. Thus none of the landscaping lasted longer than a few months and, once the runner beans had gone down with the frost and the annuals had collapsed into the mash, the whole garden disappeared, reverting to the two oblongs divided by the rubble path and reminding me of a stage with the scenery suddenly removed.

The seats, stranded in the wide-open spaces, looked foolish and useless. The moles pushed up the tiles of the patio. Grandfather gathered the tiles and stacked them behind the woodshed.

'I dunno as I wants they,' he said. 'I haven't time for fancy pavements. Nor nobody else neither. Who's got the time to sit about on fancy pavements I'd like to know. What do you think about it, then, Nell?'

Granny didn't really know. Fancy patios, which in any case she couldn't really see, meant little.

'You do as you think fit, Will,' she said. 'It'll suit me, whatever you do.'

'You're the boss,' Grandfather reminded her.

She made no reply.

At the beginning of each season Grandfather sat by the fire with a collection of seed catalogues and worked through them, marking everything he thought he'd like to grow. All the time, he consulted Granny.

'Savoy,' he said. 'What about some more of they Savoys, Nell? I wants to put cabbage where I had the beans last year, and where I had the cabbage bed, I've a mind to have the beans. And I'll put in a few more turnips. They were good, they turnips we had last year. Didn't you think so, Nell?'

'Give me the scatters,' she said.

'You never said so.'

'No. Well, it wouldn't have done any good.'

He considered what she'd told him. Then he said:

'I don't reckon as it could have bin the turnips. It was summat you picked up in the air, more like. There's any amount going about in the air, springtimes.'

'But I shan't eat no more turnips,' she said decisively. 'You grow 'em, if you want to. There's nothing to stop you and George having 'em if they agrees with you.'

He consulted the catalogue.

'We'll have some more brock-lo. I likes brock-lo. And that beet we had last year. We'll have some more of that. Good for yer blood, beet is. What do you think about that, then, Matilda?'

'It didn't do *my* blood much good. Too rich or summat.'

'Well, there's no sense in eating what rounds on you, that's for sure. What about carrots? They be all right. You can eat carrots all right, can't you Nell?'

'Yes. I can eat carrots. And I likes a mess of peas. We could do with some more peas, couldn't we, Will?'

7

'Gives you the wind, Nell . . .' he reminded her.

'Yes I know they do. But I dunno as I mind if you don't.'

He went on studying the lists and suddenly he said:

'I'm going to have a pit-light this year. We could do with a pit-light. I could fix it up out of they winders they took out of the Old Rectory last week. Make a nice pit-light they would. Bring the stuff on a treat.'

Sooner or later the planning exhausted him and he dropped back into the chair and fell asleep. In his dreams there were flowers. The marrows swelled and the postman looked over the garden wall and wanted to know how anyone could grow marrows like it . . .

Along the borders, each side of the rubble path, he put the bedding plants. He liked showy ones which grew easily and filled the garden with scent and colour. He chose pansies, violas, petunias, night scented stock, marigolds and asters; at the back of these he had gladioli, Canterbury bells, love-lies-bleeding, lupins and phlox. In the late summer there were great clumps of dahlias and Michaelmas daisies.

All through the season there were roses. He found space for them everywhere. There were ordinary ones, the sweet-smelling kind, with the big, cabbage-fat blossoms, smoking with colour. He named the different varieties with authority, Madame Plain, Grace Darling, Mrs Herbert Stevens, Melody and Shower of Gold. There were also ramblers, trained against the cottage, over archways and along rustic trellis work. There were pale pink single ones which smelled sweet and fell apart at a touch. There were those that hung in clusters like minute powder-puffs, and the big, dark pink, single ones with petals spread wide like butterfly wings in the sunshine.

Along the bank bordering the boundary was a row of gooseberry bushes. Grandfather never bothered to prune them and they formed a dense hedge belligerent with spikes. It was impossible to reach any of the fruit and the small orbs hung within, in the green shade till they dropped off into the weeds.

There were blackcurrants and they received more care. They grew by the path which branched at right angles to the rubble one and, as far as any of us knew, they had been growing there for ever. Defying the gardening books, threat of big-bud, orthodox methods of pruning and the inevitable advice from other gardeners, Grandfather dealt with them as he felt inclined. He just cut out what got in his way and left the rest to chance. Each year there was a miraculous and magnificent crop of fruit. Great bunches of berries hung like grapes, smelling of wine and warmth.

Aunt Georgie descended on the harvest with enthusiasm and made jam and puddings endlessly. Granny insisted that plenty of jam was made every year. Blackcurrants were full of nourishment, she said, and they were good for sore throats. She liked a spoonful of the jam in hot water when she had a cold coming and she offered the brew as a precaution to anyone who sniffed in her hearing.

Aunt Georgie's jam making was a process of her own. She ignored the cookery books just as Grandfather ignored gardening books. She carried the fruit into the house and tossed it straight into the saucepan along with the sugar and water and stirred it till it boiled. She never dreamed of weighing or washing it first. When it came to the boil, she left it and only returned when she had a moment to spare from whatever else she had started doing.

Left unattended, it rumbled about in the saucepan, heaving like purple lava. Sometimes a burst exploded from the centre and great blurps of it leapt the side of the pan, running down onto the stove, splattering out to the cupboard door, the floor, the walls and the ceiling. It wasn't long before the smell of burning filled the house.

9

Blue smoke misted from under the saucepan and wove into the furniture.

'You bin and burnt the jam again, then, George?' asked Granny. She came slowly into the kitchen, her nostrils twitching and her lips curling.

'A little ran over the sides, that's all. It's all right, Mum.'

'You ent boiling it too long, be you then, George? We wants ter be able ter eat it, don't we? And yer father carries on so, when the jam's tough.'

Aunt Georgie's jam was never just right. It either dripped off the bread in thin streams, or it was as solid and rubbery as toffee.

The over-cooking made a lot of extra work. Often the saucepans were absolutely ruined. If there was any hope for them, they remained for days, soaking under the sink or out in the back yard where they collected earwigs, leaves and, if left long enough, the wriggling larvae of mosquitoes. Aunt Georgie always did her best to get the burnt jam off. She chipped and scrubbed, scraped and rubbed. But if it was impossible she didn't grieve. She gave it up and said it'd be easier to get a new saucepan.

'There's plenty more where that one came from,' she said with light-hearted resignation. 'There's always plenty of old saucepans at jumble sales.'

Just beyond the currants, there was a patch of ground which Grandfather had never bothered to cultivate. Here stood the privy, leaning against the back of the old washhouse. There were nettles, brambles and ground elder. Pits were dug for emptying the privy buckets and for chucking away the old tins. There was also a huge cinder heap, rising out of the nettles like an extinct volcano.

From the centre of this weedy jungle grew the old russet apple tree. It was incredibly old, with a great gnarled trunk, scabby with age. The bark was covered

The old apple tree

with moss and lichen and it was liberally studded with
nails and bits of bent iron for holding clothes lines, water-

cans and garden oddments. A few feet from the ground the trunk divided into a huge Y. Then the two limbs headed for the sky in straight shafts and were topped with a vast matting of twigs. A mere trickle of sap moved up to nourish the leaves and the September crop of apples was small. But they were sweet and hard as nuts, brown as autumn leaves and they smelled of the sun.

The soil in the garden was black, with the texture of pudding and the quality of peat. It had grown rich with the years and with the refuse thrown into it for generations. The ash of bonfires, the contents of privy buckets, old cabbage leaves, rusty nails and tins, bones, the bodies of family cats and dogs; all had contributed to this rich, fertile loam.

And it was full of things; the treasures that never rotted and which remained hidden until turned up into the light with a spade or hoe. There were bits of twisted metal, tins in the last stage of rust so that they fell apart at a touch, leaving their two rims collapsed on the soil like rough bracelets dug from a tomb. There were numerous ginger-beer bottles, honey pots and strange dark blue and green fluted bottles with the word 'Poison' in relief at the base.

Aunt Georgie was absolutely terrified of these. She said you never knew if there was anything left in them. They were dangerous and it worried her to death, knowing they were lying about where the vegetables grew.

'Anything might have been in them,' she wailed.

'Stritch Neen,' said Granny positively when she heard that one of the bottles had been dug up. Her dull, almost sightless eyes bulged with alarm.

'Arsenic, more like,' said Grandfather, with relish.

'Don't touch 'em. Don't nobody touch 'em,' Granny cried, and Aunt Georgie said the only thing to do was to throw them in the pit where they'd be out of everybody's way for ever.

'And then you go and wash yer hands, for the love of Heaven,' Granny said. 'They frighten me to death, they old bottles do.'

Yet those bottles were beautiful. They glinted with jewel lights and their beauty seemed to me to be greater because they were supposed to be dangerous.

The soil turning also produced smaller treasures: glass beads, marbles, buttons and fragments of clay pipes. Most of these appeared only after rain, when the soil had washed off them and they'd dried light and clean in the sun. Then the minute limbs of broken dolls, fragments of floral china, tiny lead animals, the rusty keys of sardine tins and the glass eyes of toys that had long been discarded, showed up too.

There was never anything of value. No treasure trove. Nothing but ordinary, cottage garden relics that were not ancient enough to be valued or collected. So they lay on the earth for the season and then were all dug back in again and disappeared until they were turned to the light once more.

Grandfather was extremely proud of his garden. He showed everyone round. Travellers calling at the workshop to sell paint were invited to come and have a look. Aunt Georgie's village friends, who had gardens of their own, were taken to see the sights. The postman, the milkman, the baker, people passing in the lane, were all treated to conducted tours and left laden with vegetables, thinnings from the carrot row, bagfuls of beans and bunches of flowers.

The visitors who turned up too often on a Sunday were taken round each time they came. As soon as tea was finished, Grandfather began to get restless. Looking pointedly at the clock, he said that if they didn't come soon and have a look round, it would be time to go.

'I want you to come and see my roses,' he would say,

'and the beans have come on like anything since you were here last. Regular nice beans they are. Long as yer arm. Come on out and have a look at 'em . . .'

He put on his hat and led the way, up the garden path, discussing every growing thing in sight. The guests sauntered along behind, listening and looking, admiring and exclaiming, while Grandfather paused to tweak at a weed or pinch a greenfly.

'What a lovely show!' they cried. 'Did you ever see anything like it! It's glorious! What a crop of vegetables! It's your green thumbs, that's what it is, Uncle Bill! It must be your green thumbs!'

'And it ent only me thumbs what be green,' said Grandfather. 'I be pretty well green all over, according to some.'

Exclamations and comments drifted in the air and he was pleased. He knew he deserved praise and responded happily.

A favourite visitor was Mabel Berry. He showed her everything from the beans to the new seats.

'Come on, set yerself on that along o' me,' he said. 'It's a regular nice seat and you're a regular nice gal. . . . I be past any nonsense so come and set along o' me and enjoy the view.'

Mabel had a small garden of her own in the town where she lived. But it was minute and she battled with soot and fumes. She envied our clean country gardens and wished hers was open to the wind and the weather. Now, during her Sunday visits, she walked with Grandfather, picking her way carefully in her tight, white summer shoes.

'You're a real marvel, Uncle Bill,' she told him. 'Look at those asters! Mine aren't half the size of yours! When did you say you put them in? And—oh, I say! That's done well, hasn't it? No bigger than my little finger when I saw it last. You've bin spitting on it again, I suppose!'

'I never said as I spits on it . . .'

'That's what you said. That's what you told me last time I was here. "Spits on it every morning and last thing at night," you said.'

'Well, you can't believe everything *I* say,' Grandfather told her. 'Here, you come on and have a look at my peas.'

There was silence in the garden for a time. Later, the voices began to drift from somewhere else . . .

'Uncle Bill!' squealed Mabel. Her voice was shrill as a bird's and keen with protest. 'That's enough . . . quite, quite enough! What d'you think you're doing? What's Aunt Matilda going to say when *she* finds out what you're up to!'

'You be my favourite gal. Now be thankful for small mercies,' said Grandfather.

We all knew he was giving the vegetables away again . . .

The visitors always left laden with produce. And they always promised to come and see us again soon.

'They'll come all right. I'd stake my last penny on that!' said Father. 'Where else could they get all that grub thrown at 'em the way they do here?'

Grandfather agreed. Once they'd gone, his spontaneous generosity changed to regret that he'd given away so much.

'It's a bit of all right,' he told Granny. 'They folks comes here Sunday after Sunday, expecting what they'll get, and they never gives a thought to what it costs we in seed and the time to grow the stuff. Take that chap we had here last Sunday. Would've taken the old apple tree as well, if he'd had half a chance . . . didn't know whether he'd got runner beans or peas in the bag. Doesn't know the difference between his arse and a hole in the ground. Nell! Did you hear what I just said?'

'Yes I did. And I wasn't listening. You goes too far sometimes in what you says, Will.'

From time to time he grew something out of the

ordinary, like asparagus or Madonna lilies. Since no one really cared for the asparagus, it evolved into a ferny thicket which was used for adding greenery to vases of sweet peas. The lilies made a slow start and never came to anything until he planted them at the back of the yellow privet hedge by the privy. A more unsuitable place he could not have found, but they thrived. They grew into vigorous plants with huge buds, loaded with promise. Later their white bells spread and hung like small, fancy lampshades in the shadows.

'Just you look at they lilies!' said Grandfather. 'Did you ever see anything to touch 'em? According to the book they oughter be dead. That soil is no good to 'em it says. But look at 'em blooming away like one o'clock!'

One morning Mr Daley from the farm cottages called. His sister had just died and he wanted to talk to Grandfather about the funeral arrangements. Grandfather was out, but Aunt Georgie promised to give him the message the moment he got back.

'I've been looking at your lilies,' said Mr Daley. 'I was wondering if you wanted them.'

'Want them! They're the pride of Father's life!' cried Aunt Georgie.

'Then I was wondering if he'd be good enough to spare one or two for my poor sister's coffin. So fond of lilies, she was. And there isn't a lily to be bought in the place.'

Aunt Georgie hesitated, pink with confusion.

'I wouldn't be after asking favours if it wasn't for the dead, God rest her soul . . .'

Aunt Georgie said she really didn't know about cutting lilies. But if they were for the dead . . .

She went indoors and fetched her scissors.

When Grandfather returned the first thing he noticed was the lily bed.

'Where be my lilies?' he demanded. 'George! Where

be my lilies? What's happened to my lilies? Who's bin
and cut my lilies down?'

When she told him, he took one more look at the bloom-
less spikes by the privet hedge and went into the sitting-
room and sat down.

'I'll come home and find the roof gone next,' he said.

'What be wrong then Will?' asked Granny.

Grandfather told her.

'And I know that fellow. Everybody knows him. Won't
spend twopence if he can save it. Talks his way to getting
anything he fancies. And now he's had my lilies and all
because the bugger's too mean to pay for a wreath . . .
well, I'll have 'em put on the bill along with the coffin
and everything else. And I'll see he's charged dear . . .'

Granny sat for a while, thinking it over. Then she said:

'It ent right, no more it ent. Straight, you don't know
what people are going to do next, do you, Will?'

2

The rest of the family did not like gardening very much. Father regarded it merely as a means of producing cheap vegetables for the family. He planted a supply of the same ones every year, at the same time, regardless of season, soil and weather conditions.

He had a set idea that there must be spring cabbage cut for Whit Monday whether Whitsun was early or late. He worried if others in the village picked their peas before he did, particularly if they had planted them later. When Mother told him that it didn't matter, because it simply meant we'd be having peas later, perhaps long after everyone else's had finished, he wasn't convinced. What mattered most was having them first and early.

He worried when our brussels sprouts got club root: and they got it every year.

'Bloody things! They've got it again!' he announced, surveying the rows of young plants, drooping in the sun. 'Look at 'em! Been in a month and by the look of 'em you'd think I only put 'em in yesterday.'

It wasn't any good telling him about the life cycle of the fly and its grub which caused the cancerous growth.

'We always used to grow good sprouts there,' he argued, and he wasn't interested in the life cycle of any fly.

Mother's philosophical attitude and indifference to competition actually made him worse. He had his fixed ideas and opinions and didn't like them challenged. I could never understand why he made such a fuss. We always seemed to have plenty of beans and peas and sprouts despite the disasters and the proclamations of doom.

Mother took over the flowers, but she was a hopeless

gardener with no touch for plants and absolutely no instinct for growing anything at all. She couldn't handle a spade, and when she used a hoe she cut everything down. She confused weeds with the plants she had just set out and it was always a gamble whether there'd be anything left to bloom.

I liked growing mustard and cress on flannel in a saucer in the kitchen and she saw this as an opportunity to hand over the garden, convincing me that I had green fingers. Not only that, my back was younger and I didn't have so far to bend down.

Her only real success in the garden was achieved long before my sisters and I were born. She had once decided, she said, to grow marigolds, because you couldn't go wrong with them, and they made a good show. She sowed a few packets of seed and from then on the garden was never without them. They sprang up, vigorous and strong each year, out of the borders, along the sides of the paths and out of the walls. Sometimes a stray one turned up among the beans and carrots. Sometimes they bloomed in the hedge on the opposite side of the lane where someone had deposited a basketful of weeds.

But if Mother was a ham-fisted gardener, Aunt Georgie was a great deal worse. She also had no instinct about plants. She scarcely knew a primrose from a buttercup, yet for some reason, suddenly decided she must have a garden of her own. She chose a strip of ground along the north side of the old wash house, right by the path to the privy. It was easily the most unsuitable place in the whole garden and caught all the drips from the wash-house roof. It had no sun and the earth was eternally damp and cold and covered with brilliant green moss.

She dug primroses from the woods and set them in a row and they did well for a time. When they were over she planted forget-me-nots, which rapidly developed a shrivelled sickly appearance and turned pale grey.

'They forget-me-nots,' remarked Grandfather on his way to the privy, 'they don't look any too good, George. Got the blight by the look of it. That's what be wrong with they. Blight. Regular bilious they be.'

One day her friend, Mrs Wells, gave her some rock rose cuttings to replace them. A show of rock roses would be nice, she said. But they didn't do so well, either. They seemed to pause there in the damp little bed. No new leaves appeared. The ones already out withered and curled.

Aunt Georgie drenched them with water and scooped new horse dung from the lane. It was still warm. It looked rich and green and she thought it would do some good.

When Mrs Wells called in for a cup of tea a few days later, she asked after the cuttings.

'They don't seem any too good,' said Aunt Georgie.

'They'll take time to pick up,' said Mrs Wells.

Aunt Georgie led her to the little black border.

'They're upside down!' said Mrs Wells. 'You've put them in upside down, Georgie! It's too late to do anything about them. They're too far gone. They're dead as nits!'

'Well I never! Would you believe it!'

Aunt Georgie stood looking at them with mild surprise. That was her final attempt at gardening. She pulled up the shrivelled remains and never tried again.

At the far end of Grandfather's garden was an enormous yew tree. Like a great green palace, it spread its dark whispering foliage far out over the garden. Amid the branches the light was a dappled confusion of sunlight and reflections, streaked with pink and gold. The limbs were purple and crimson and the shadows where the foliage was thickest were black and dense.

I often climbed to the top and lay along a branch to listen to the wind and the birds and feel the sway of the foliage and the isolation of such a remote place. The people in the garden below were far away. Their voices were indistinct. They were part of another world, which, while I was up here, did not concern me. From between the leaves the garden looked small and without mystery, for it was possible to see it all at once. Everything was visible, like a map in patches of green divided by thin paths and rows of cabbages.

The two cottages stood far off, diminished, like toys, with people the size of dolls going in and out of them. Granny, on the pitchen, reminded me of a black beetle crawling in the sun. The flashing colour of Aunt Georgie's summer dress seemed to be the passing of a butterfly. Grandfather stood, pondering over the flowers like a garden statue. My mother, far beyond the yellow privet hedge, busied about with washing and potato peelings and stood sharpening her cooking knife on the doorstep.

I thought it was the most beautiful tree in the world. It was the largest and greenest, the sturdiest and the most magnificent. It was royal and superior, a thing of extraordinary excellence. It had been growing for hundreds of years and it was certain that it would continue to grow for hundreds more . . .

Then, early one morning, tragically and unexpectedly it was doomed.

Five cows escaped from Butcher's Lands, opposite the cottage, and found their way into Grandfather's garden. As Aunt Georgie looked out from her bedroom window while dressing, she saw them, trampling about in a circle beneath the tree.

'Father!' she screamed. 'Father, there's cows in the garden! Dozens of them, all round the old yew tree, eating their heads off!'

Everyone was alerted and we rushed out.

We saw the damage at once. The lawn was pitted with deep hoof marks. The flowerbeds were trampled. The roses had been bitten off and the cabbages were eaten.

Such havoc had never before occurred in the garden. Mother, always good in a crisis, was quick to assess what should be done. We were to form a half-circle and force the cows towards the gate. As we closed in on them, she ordered us to walk slowly: not to panic and not to shout.

Then father came rushing out, pulling on his trousers. 'Get out of there!' he shouted. 'Get out of it; get out of it!'

He chucked lumps of soil and hit them in the flanks so that they leapt with surprise and took off into the cabbages in hysterical plunges.

'For goodness' sake, Fred, stop shouting at them. You're making them worse! Just as I'd got them where I wanted them . . . now look at them! All over the place again. . . . Now, all of you, spread out again, and move towards them slowly, and *don't* shout . . .'

Father dropped back and stood sucking his teeth, the haze of sleep still in his eyes.

Mother's tactics succeeded and the cows formed a small group and trotted into the lane.

'Keep following them,' she said. 'Keep on following behind till they're right out of the way. Ten to one, they'll make for the place they broke out of . . .'

After everyone had made a survey of the damage, it was Granny who began to worry about the cows.

'They might have all been poisoned if they'd eaten that old yew tree,' she said, shocked by the vision that had suddenly hit her. 'Do you think they had much of it then, Will?'

'Not by the look of my cabbage bed, they didn't. Eaten pretty well all of it, they have. And been trampling over my borders half the night by the look of them. Made a proper mess of my garden they have.'

'It'd be terrible if they got in again and had some more of that yew,' Granny persisted. 'I don't like it, Will.

That old tree, I mean. Poisonous stuff, yew. Kill anything it will. And I shouldn't wonder if it didn't poison the ground. Taints the cabbage I shouldn't wonder. And we bin eating it for donkey's years and never given it a thought.'

'It'd cost summat to replace all they cows if anything went wrong,' said Grandfather.

'But it wouldn't be our funeral, would it, Will?' asked Granny. Suddenly her lips were pale.

'I dunno so much. Liability's a funny business. We never shuts our gate, Nell. Bin off its hinges these last five year. But whether it's our funeral or not, I dunno as we wants to fall out with the farmers. We get a lot of work off them round here, we do, Nell.'

So the decision to have the tree cut was made. Grandfather wasted no time and two men arrived one evening with a cross saw and a bag of wedges. We all went out to watch, not because we wanted to, but because we were caught up in the compulsion of something horrific.

As the first chips flew all I could think was that I would never be climbing into the top branches again, never again be able to retreat into the centre of that great, green whispering world.

Swinging their axes, sawing with concentration, the men paused from time to time to knock in a wedge.

'Bloody hard wood, yew,' remarked Father. He was staring at the trunk, sucking his teeth.

'Hard as iron,' said Grandfather. He was sitting on an up-turned bucket, smoking a pipe.

'For goodness' sake, you children, keep out of the way when it falls,' said Mother. 'It'll come right out to the path, I expect. There's no knowing how far the branches will come.'

The light was beginning to fade when the tree shivered. The first shudder went through it in a shock which rippled out into the branches.

'It won't be long now,' said Father. The rest of us could say nothing. Something important was going on and we couldn't talk about it.

Suddenly there was a pause. The tree, the men, the garden, the whole world seemed to hesitate. Then down it went. With a splintering crack and a twist of despair, it plunged with every twig snapping and the foliage sinking. The sliced trunk opened red to the sky like a brilliant, bloodless wound.

I looked at the great thing and knew that something absolutely terrible had been done. . . .

We all drew near, like hunters inspecting a kill. None of us spoke. There was still nothing we could possibly say. Granny, who had been waiting in the house, listening for the sound of the fall, at last emerged.

'Got the old tree down, then,' she said, breaking into the silence like somebody talking loudly in a church.

She moved towards it, treading cautiously as if she was afraid she'd fall into it. No one stepped forward to guide her.

'It came down a treat,' said Grandfather, for she had broken the spell for him.

I looked at them, not understanding their lack of feeling.

It was so unlike them to accept such a dramatic change, to be willing to abolish something that had been such a part of their world for so long.

'Half my stummick trouble has been on account of that old tree, I shouldn't wonder,' Granny went on. 'It stands to reason, Will. It taints everything round it.'

'It'd poison my Granny's old cat,' murmured Grandfather.

There were unfamiliar horizons in the garden now, more daylight and a blue expanse above which seemed to stretch to the limits of space. There was no long afternoon shadow falling across the garden, and the privy, which had stood behind the trunk, was exposed.

'Look at it!' wailed Aunt Georgie. 'A fine sight *that* makes from the road, and no mistake!'

'Everybody knows what it is,' said Grandfather indifferently. 'Everybody has to have one o' they, of one sort or another.'

'That's not the point. It doesn't look nice all exposed for everyone passing up and down the lane to see.'

'Then there's no need for 'em to look at it,' said Grandfather. 'They've no business to be looking in on other people's property. Besides, it ent used except for storing my bean sticks and what's wrong with the sight of a shed where I stores my bean sticks, I don't know!'

In a few weeks, the first shoots from an elder bush which had lain dormant in the overpowering shade of the yew, began to show. They grew rapidly and it wasn't long before a whole tree had developed, spraying its long green branches before the old privy. By the end of the summer only the roof was visible from the road.

That same year, the old russet apple tree fell. It happened on a summer day, with no wind. Calm and warm, with a metal-blue sky and dust on the border plants, it was a day no one would have dreamed that the old tree was ready to go. Without even a crack of warning, it began to sway. Then, gently and deliberately, like an old man stumbling with heart failure, it collapsed.

Mother was leaning from the bedroom window watching the garden, and the unexpected movement caught her eye. She knew what was about to happen.

'Children!' she shrieked. 'Look at the old apple tree! Call Aunt Georgie! Everyone look at the old apple tree! It's falling . . . it's falling over!'

Even as she screamed, it toppled and settled into the currant bushes, crushing the summit of the cinder heap as it fell.

There was no sound except for the rustle of disturbed twigs, and there was vast space of vacant sky where it had been.

'Well I be buggered!' said Grandfather. 'Fancy that old tree cocking over like that! Must be old age, mu'nt it?'

He was the only one who spoke. The rest of us stood and stared, gazing at it as if one of the family had dropped dead.

We could see how huge it was and how rotten its trunk had become. It was hollow right up to where it branched, and the inside was lined with flakes of dead wood. It was a miracle that it had stood up for so long; a greater miracle that it had resisted winter gales and the blustery March winds. The great shaggy top-knot of twigs, now sprawled among the bushes, was now more than ever like some vast bird's nest.

We saw all the things that had lodged in it, things blown by the wind, the washing torn from the line, toys thrown up by children, an old doll which had been dangling by one leg for years, like a miniature sun-bleached corpse.

There were the remains of a pair of navy-blue knickers in delicate, grey-green shreds, as rotten as old moss. There were bits of wood, tins, handkerchiefs, a coil of wire, an old sock, dozens of old nests.

'It might have pitched down and killed us stone dead as we hung out the washing,' said Granny fearfully. 'Reely O, it's properly upset my stummick it has, and no mistake.'

'Go on in and have a drop of brandy and a sit down, then, Mum,' advised Aunt Georgie. 'There's no sense stopping out here, imagining what might have happened.'

When the heat of the day had gone, Grandfather set to work on the old tree with a bill-hook and saw.

'Brittle as dust, it is,' he said to Granny later. 'I just touched one o' they branches and it crumbled off in my hands. Not a drop o' sap in it. What kept it alive I don't know.'

'When I thinks about it, standing there, ready to go, I feel quite faint,' she said. 'I bin setting here all day and thinking if one o' they little children happened to be running under it when it went over, they'd never have stood a chance. No more they would.'

I went out to look at it late in the evening. Grandfather had done all he meant to do. The twigs lay in a heap ready for burning. The hulk lay abandoned across the cinder heap. Dark brown dust had flowed from the shuck into the cavity where it had been rooted. There were beetles and woodlice scurrying as if they had only just been disturbed.

There were curious white grubs lying raw in the light with the beetles and centipedes. I put my hand into a hole in the trunk, a hole which had been too far off the ground to reach. It had always been a favourite nesting place for starlings. It was packed with moss and dried grass; soft, warm, yielding and bone dry, and my fingers closed over a clutch of eggs. There were five.

I drew one out and held it in my palm. It was still warm, vivid blue in the twilight. It was an exquisite thing, an unexpected treasure, and it lay like a smooth, luminous pebble, the last of the season, doomed with the tree.

3

Just as the grass in Grandfather's garden was greener, the apples were sweeter and the flowers brighter and bigger, so his privy was infinitely superior to ours. It was far better hidden and it was smaller. It had been built discreetly on to the back of the old stone wash-house and no one could have guessed it was there. The corrugated iron roof, painted brown, sat on brick walls and there was a frosted glass window which faced south. The sun shone through it most of the day and cast a square of golden light on to the floor. A thick green honeysuckle hedge camouflaged the entrance. There was a crimson flowering currant mingled with orange blossom on the wall below the window and a yellow privet hedge along the path to the door. The path was gravelled and thick moss grew among the stones.

The privy was whitewashed inside. Grandfather did it every August Bank Holiday. The seat was kept scrubbed and had become almost as white as the walls. The wood was soft, polished by use and warm to the touch in any weather. There were two wooden buttons holding the front panel in place where the bucket slid in and out. The floor had a scrap of coloured matting and there was a pile of newspapers on a ledge. There were also a roll of Bronco and a bottle of Jeyes' Fluid which gave a strong hygienic odour to the place.

It was light and sunny inside. The feeling of the garden was all around, with the sound of the wind in the apple trees and the songs of the birds in the hedge. In the summer, the warmth of the sun penetrated the iron roof and there was the sound of sparrows hopping on it, and the padding of the cats as they made their way towards the

Grandfather's privy

wash-house roof, where they slept against the chimney-stack.

The roof in autumn was bombed by little apples from

the old russet tree and the wind caught at the currant bush and swept its twigs against the window, backwards and forwards, squeaking over the surface; and the sound was like mice communicating with each other in the garden.

Our privy was gloomy, a windowless place built of dark stone with thick walls and a steeply pitched tile roof. It lurked under the thick foliage of an ancient Portuguese laurel with twisting limbs like monstrous snakes. During wet weather these shapes turned darker with the rain, streaked and dripping, they appeared to writhe in the storm, seeking the support of the privy roof and adding to the terrors of the place. The walls were distempered only when there was some left over from something else. But Mother sometimes threatened to paint them herself, which was a sure way of getting them done.

Father preferred to do it even though he wasn't particular about technique, and gathered mildew, cobwebs and dust along with the brush as he worked.

'What could you have better than that!' he said when he'd done. 'Look's a treat. Sweet as a nut. Fit for a duchess!'

Whatever the weather, the place was filled with shadows. It was haunted by rats and beetles and there were mysterious noises in the roof. Ivy and hop had worked in under the tiles to form a web of twigs and tendrils. The laurel branches creaked and the door winced as it strained against its rickety latch. Everything contributed to the eternal, sinister mood.

The seat was plain wood, but it was never scrubbed and it had grown dark with age. The sides were done over with Church Oak Varnish which gave them a metallic sheen. This scratched easily and there were always telltale marks left by cats and rats which had scrambled up its sides. There were newspapers on the seat, but no luxuries like Bronco and Jeyes' Fluid. Mother said these things were too expensive and, in any case, she hadn't the money to buy things to throw away.

However, there was a toilet roll holder on the door. It was called 'The Reliable' and had two hands, exquisitely shaped, clasped beneath the spring of the holder. The door of our privy was painted brown and opened outwards. Mother looked at Father when she remarked that a lunatic must have hung it . . .

I hated this privy. I wished it was light and sweet like the one next door. I used to pray that our visitors wouldn't ask to go to it. I was so ashamed of the darkness, the ivy and the cobwebs. And often, Father had forgotten to empty the bucket, or hadn't had time, and then I wished I could drop dead.

But no one else seemed to mind very much. Mother told me I was far too fussy. Everyone who lived in the country understood, and if they didn't, then it was high time they learned a few simple facts of life.

'Show Mrs So-and-so up the garden, will you dear?' she would say without any embarrassment.

Father made pointed jokes about it. He told people it was a sight better than a bush. There was a roof over your head and a paper to read, a nice, comfortable seat to sit on and what more could you want? And one of these days he was going to hang up a chain, just for the look of the thing. But if anyone had pulled it, they would have brought the roof down on their heads, handicap books and all. He kept all his old racing journals here, on the ledge beneath the roof, along with the bottles of rat poison and the break-back traps . . . a sinister collection which added to the menace of the place.

Sometimes, if he felt frivolous, he'd sing one of his songs, which always began:

'The moon shone on the Privy door . . .'

But Mother always stopped him swiftly.

'Shut up, Fred,' she said. 'No one wants to hear *that* . . .'

He often told us we were better off with our privy than he'd been when he was a boy. In those days the family used the old one which stood by the yew tree at the top of Grandfather's garden. There wasn't even a bucket then. There was just a large hole dug beneath the seat and you perched on the edge and hoped for the best. Once a year, Grandfather employed an old man from the village to come and empty it. He dug it all out with a shovel and Grandfather paid him half a crown. It was a terrible job for anyone to have to do, but the old man didn't seem to mind. His only comment when he received his pay was:

'It did *stink*, Mr Budd!'

Grandfather often said it would be nice to have a real, posh, modern flush convenience, and one of these days when he had the time and the weather was set fair, he'd see about putting one in. He asked Granny what she thought and she said she really didn't know. She didn't mind what there was, as long as there was somewhere . . .

'But what we've got is all right, ent it Will?' she asked. 'What's the matter with what we've got, eh?'

'Nothing,' he said, 'nothing's the matter with it. But I thought we might like a change. Something a bit sweeter. Something a bit more up-to-date, like.'

'I'd just as soon keep what we got,' she said. 'I knows me way about in it.'

Granny never had been an advocate of change and progress.

But I lived in the constant hope of something better. I thought enviously of the fine arrangements in the houses I'd visited: the gleaming china so aptly titled 'The Exclusive', 'The Perfection', 'The Supreme', and 'The Cascade'—white or charmingly decorated with chrysan-themums and roses, their ice-white throats breathing odours of carbolic . . .

32

Fit for a Duchess

One of Mother's friends was very nervous of privies. She'd had a bad fright in one when she was young, and had never really got over it. It happened when she was staying with friends who lived at the back of beyond. Their privy was some distance from the house, at the end of a long path. For her last visit, before bedtime, she was given a candle. There were matches in the holder and the night was windy.

'If you hold your hand round the flame it won't go out,' she was told.

Off she went, nervously into the night, shielding the flame. Just when she reached the darkest part of the garden the candle went out.

'And there I was in the pitch black. I'd dropped the matches and couldn't find them. The wind was roaring. I couldn't see any light from the house.'

She groped her way forward, not caring whether she arrived back at the house or at her destination. After a few steps, her hand closed over a door handle and she realized she had found it. The door was half open, so she pushed and went in. In the darkness, she bent slowly to where she estimated the seat would be. She landed on thick, hot fur, which shot with a shrill hiss into the night, clawing and snarling.

'I could hear it ploughing through the dead leaves. I was nearly sick. You've no idea how vulnerable you are in the middle of the night with your knickers round your ankles!'

'Of course, it was only a cat,' she added, 'but no one could have convinced me at the time. Now, even in full daylight, when I can *see* everything, I'm cautious about privies. I bang on the door and wait and take a good look at the seat before I venture in.'

Occasionally, an elderly lady who lived with her sister in a large house at the end of our lane called at the cottage on her way home from a walk on the common. This was generally about noon and when the doorbell rang, Mother said:

'That'll be Miss Hodges, I expect.'

She hurried to the door. Miss Hodges was there, standing on the doorstep like a tweed-clad ghost, holding a gold-topped cane delicately in a gloved hand. Below the heavy hem of her thick skirt, her legs were like genteel twigs. Her long face was framed by a fuzz of faded yellow hair.

'I do beg your pardon for calling on you once again, Mrs Budd,' she said in her thin, slow, cultured voice, 'but I wonder if you would be so kind as to allow me to use your lavatory?'

Each syllable was pronounced with precision and bleated through thin nostrils.

'Yes, of course, you may,' said Mother hastily. 'You do remember it's only a country one, don't you?'

'I shall not become trapped again, shall I?' said Miss Hodges.

'Not if you lift the latch and the door at the same time,' said Mother.

'How very complicated,' murmured Miss Hodges, 'and how clever of your family to manage such a problem. I do so admire you all.'

Mother didn't say that none of us ever bothered to latch the door. If we wanted anyone to know that we were there we began to sing or drum our heels on the wood.

With delicate, measured tread, Miss Hodges went up the path to the privy. She was as pale as a corpse and totally out of place in our cottage garden. We hovered where we could watch her come out, and when she emerged she re-trod the path in a gracious progress, showing no sign of what she thought about the newspapers and cobwebs.

She thanked Mother for her kindness in allowing her to take advantage of our convenience. Then she continued on her way down the lane, murmuring that she had to go or she'd be late for luncheon. Brittle as an old egg-shell, gently born and odourless, she passed through our lives like a glancing shadow.

If Father was in the house, he asked needlessly what she wanted.

'Don't ask silly questions,' said Mother.

But Father wanted to know why she didn't find a bush like anyone else if they were taken short.

'If she had to empty the bucket like I have to, she wouldn't be so keen to fill it!' he said.

4

It wasn't only the next-door privy that was better than ours. The food in Grandfather's cottage was superior also. The bread and butter tasted nicer and the milk was creamier, which wasn't really surprising because Mother sometimes put water with ours to make it go further.

There was much more sugar in Aunt Georgie's mint sauce and thicker jelly under the dripping. There were no powdery lumps in the custard and no brittle, black-varnished skin on rice puddings. Aunt Georgie was a better cook and she believed in quality rather than quantity. She didn't cover up failures by saying that children will eat anything if they are hungry enough.

Mother made fearful, solid porridge. Fried bread was inches thick. There were endless stews with hard chunks of turnip and swede; mountainous treacle puddings with only a suggestion of treacle. Often there were dishes of batter spread with cold jam. The batter had collapsed as it cooked and lay like a layer of yellow clay in the dish when it came out of the oven.

Mother made bread-and-butter pudding with thick bread smeared with margarine because she said it was a pity to waste good butter in a pudding. She pressed these chunks of bread into the dish and added random spoonfuls of jam, explaining that the heat of the oven would help to spread it. Whatever milk was to spare was tipped in and, sometimes, if there wasn't enough, she'd add a splash or two of water. Finally, the top was sprinkled with sugar and currants. The currants always got burnt and lay on top like smooth cinders in the crags of the crust. Most of the milk disappeared, but fortunately the bread remained soggy and to relieve the flavour there were traces of jam. We ate as much as we could and the rest was thrown out for the birds. The hardest and most burnt crusts lay about for days. Even the birds were not partial to them.

Mother also burned the potatoes with regularity, forgetting they were on, and it was only the bitter-sweet scent of their burning that reminded her.

'The potatoes! Oh, the potatoes!' she cried. She rushed to snatch the saucepan from the flame. Holding it before her, she advanced to the sink and flung it, shimmering with the vapours of hot metal and scorching food, under the tap. As the cold water beat down, there was a scream of steam. A column of smoke rose to the ceiling, curved round the dresser, along the ceiling and out of the door.

When it thinned, and the hissing stopped, Mother inspected the potatoes and decided whether they were fit to eat. She poured off the water and lifted the unburnt bits from their bed of carbon. Laying them optimistically on a plate, she doused them with salt and pepper and said no one would ever guess . . . but she didn't fool any of us.

She burnt the cakes too. Every batch of little ones had a black rim and some had a charcoal base as well. The big, family fruit cakes, which were intended to last a week, were reduced in size to less than half because so much had to be scraped off. The tops were covered with black, brittle orbs which had once been raisins, tough, rubbery and impossible to chew.

At some time every baking day, Mother would be standing on the back doorstep, scraping away at the latest cake, with the black grit flying in a storm around her.

And no one on earth had such burnt sausages as we had. Fat and soft enough when they were put into the pan, they were soon reduced to small, oblong cinders, emitting a pale blue vapour and as shiny as if they had been varnished. As we stabbed them with our forks, they snapped to pieces which shot off into inaccessible places.

'Look out you don't break the windows . . .' Father muttered and Mother said:

'Leave them for the dog. He'll eat them when he finds them.'

I often wondered why she always burned the food. It seemed so easy not to. Aunt Georgie never burned hers, except perhaps the jam, which was somehow different and didn't seem to matter very much.

Her bread-and-butter puddings were masterpieces of kitchen art. Pale gold and sparkling with sugar, they were full of juicy raisins, floating about in the refined liquors of milk and butter. The dish was always well greased so the first layer of bread never stuck to the bottom and had to be soaked for days before it would chip off.

Even Aunt Georgie's gravy was better. It was thick and creamy and impregnated with all the richest flavours of the kitchen. It lay on the roast like an appetizing custard and was so different from ours, which was thin and brown and smelled of hot water.

Mother didn't like the daily routine of cooking. She had a certain flair for icing cakes and concocting fancy oddments coloured with cochineal and flavoured with almonds and synthetic rum, but was bored with the monotony of preparing potatoes and stews. She hadn't been brought up to do it and had no imagination; nor was she good at picking things up for herself. When she discovered a recipe she liked and which was within her range, she spoiled the result by forgetting it was in the oven. And then we had the same thing again and again until we were sick of the sight and smell of it.

Mother was a creature of habit. When she discovered an author she liked, she read only his or her books. Over and over again she read Edgar Wallace; over and over again she read Baroness Orczy and Gene Stratton Porter. While the craze was on I asked her if she minded re-reading something that had no more surprises. She said:

Fit for a Duchess

'What difference does it make, whether you know the end or not? You read books to take yourself out of yourself.' She didn't want to go rushing off to new places every five minutes. It was the same with books.

And it happened with fish. For a time she bought fish in Petersfield Market. In her opinion, there was no other fish like that fish. It was cheap and good and you'd have to go a long way to beat it. One day she bought some from Mrs Edwards in a nearby village. From then on we had Mrs Edwards's fish instead . . .

We got up early in time to catch the first bus on Monday morning, so that we'd be sure to be on the doorstep as the shop opened. Mrs Edwards's son Roddy was putting the fish out on the marble slab when we arrived.

'Good mornings, Mrs Budds,' said Roddy. He always spoke in the plural. He was plump and good-natured and Mother thought he was probably a bit simple. He had a pink face and minute ears, flat against his head like little shells. Mother said they looked as if they'd been trained to lie flat with sticking plaster, when he was a baby. His teeth looked exactly like a row of tiny beads. He cycled about the district all day long, the front wheel of his bicycle lurching from side to side and his brown, un-buttoned overall flapping like calico wings.

When Mrs Edwards heard Mother arriving she emerged hastily from her private room at the back of the shop, still in her dressing-gown and slippers. She liked a Monday morning gossip with Mother, for Mother sympathized with her so readily. She emerged slowly; magnificent, bleary with sleep and smelling of warm beds and embro-cation. There were pale, swollen bags beneath her eyes and the gums of her false teeth looked brilliant pink against her pale face.

Through a curtain, which parted as she came out, there was a glimpse of a mahogany sideboard piled with china and washing. There were a canary cage covered with a chintz cloth, a dark red velvet table cloth and her elderly husband, sitting, collarless, in an easy chair. As she moved, she brought with her the odours of a breakfast fry, the bird cage and paraffin.

'We've only just managed to get Roddy's collections put away,' she said. 'I said to him, I said, "Look at that clock, Roddy! It's Monday morning and Mrs Budd'll be here in a minute and you haven't started to put your birds' eggs away!" I said to him.'

Roddy kept a collection of birds' eggs and cigarette cards on the marble fish slab during the weekends. I never could understand why.

Mrs Edwards wrapped Mother's fish in newspaper and gave her a run-down on the news.

'Mr Edwards was poorly again . . . the peke had a stoppage and I had to get the vet to it . . . one of the canaries died. . . . I wish Roddy would stop messing about with birds' eggs and cigarette cards and get himself a girl . . . Your change, Mrs Budd . . . six and three is nine and nine is eighteen pence . . . yes, I do worry about Roddy so. He's getting on for forty now, you know, and he just doesn't seem to show any interest in getting married. I get so anxious about him. I tell him, he won't always have his Mum to look after him.'

I stood by and listened to these gloomy conversations, watching the parcel of fish growing dark and wet, watching Roddy set off on his morning round, and seeing Mr Edwards come creaking out to serve the customers so that his wife could go and dress herself.

'Well, I'll be in again next Monday, all being well,' said Mother with sudden cheerfulness. 'Take care of yourself, Mrs Edwards. Good morning. Good morning to you, Mr Edwards.'

After Mrs Edwards's fish we fed on fish cakes for a time. They were a nice change at first and then we grew tired of them. They seemed to lose their taste.

'There's not much fish about them,' Father remarked one day as he pulled a bone from his mouth. 'The rest's potato as far as I can make out.'

Mother sighed, admitting they weren't as good as they were. She said she wouldn't get any more.

A feeling of relief flowed into me. I wondered what we'd get in place of them. . . .

Mother had an absolute passion for cream cakes. When we went shopping she paused to gaze at the rows of oozing pastry concoctions, wondering if she could run to a few, and which to have and whether the ones in the shop round the corner might be bigger and better and cheaper. She bought them exclusively for herself, as a treat, she said, to make up for all the other things she did without.

' Of course, I really oughtn't to eat them with my figure,' she said, though we knew that her figure didn't interest her.

She chose her cream cakes with care, pointing with her little finger delicately crooked, to the ones she fancied and pausing with that same crooked little finger resting thoughtfully against her lips as she considered what to have next. At home she settled down to eat them, withdrawing into a private gluttonous world in which she was not called upon to share anything with anyone. Biting into the side of a cream bun, with her eyes closed in ecstasy, the cream was squeezed out and frothed on to her cheeks. Then suddenly she opened her eyes, flicked her face with her fingers and licked them clean.

As if to atone for her spell of greed, she announced that we could do whatever we liked, the whole afternoon was ours . . . and we'd all go down to the hanger and pick flowers for the cottage hospital.

' Leave everything just as it is!' she ordered as she rose from the dinner table and dived into the cellar to find enough baskets. She hurried next door to tell Aunt Georgie that we were going out for the afternoon and would she mind keeping an eye on the fire.

It was primrose time and we went to the hanger beyond the meadows at the bottom of our garden. There the primroses grew in drifts, pale moon-yellow smudges thrusting through the brown leaves, as thick as buttercups in the summer grass. There were also anemones and masses of early purple orchids which smelled of tom cats and which Mother avoided, asking us not to pick any because no one wanted that smell brought to their bedsides.

'But you can pick some for Granny if you want to,' she added. 'Granny won't care about the smell of cats.'

We knelt in the deep, dry leaves and plucked flowers all afternoon. Overhead the spring twigs rattled in the wind and the birds sang. Long shadows from the still bare tree trunks ran over the ground and the dead leaves were tinted with pink and gold. Crouching alone in our chosen patch, we had nothing to say. The afternoon passed in a drift of pleasure.

Back home later, the draining board was stacked with dirty dishes and saucepans. Abandoned dinner plates littered the table. The smell of stew filled the house; the cold, meaty odour unpleasant after the clean, sun-scented woods.

Mother quickly set us to work.

'All of you,' she said briskly, her leisurely mood of the woods and her leniency gone, 'quickly, I want it all cleared and put away before your father comes in. You know what he says if he finds dirty dinner things still on the table!'

She hurried about, stacking plates and gathering cutlery into heaps. She put on the kettle, cut bread and butter and crammed the primroses into a bowl, all, it seemed, at the same time.

Each of us got on with a job without any discussion, got in each other's way, tripped over one another, collided with Mother . . . but nothing mattered, and everything was forgiven, in the mad race to get done in time. We were all dedicated to a common cause.

With the same enthusiasm that she announced the trip to pick flowers, she told us all that we were going to watch a wedding. Actually, she was not particularly interested in weddings, but this one was different. It was really big, one of the major events that no one could ignore. The daughter of a well-known resident was marrying the son of a well-known resident of a neighbouring village. Hundreds of guests had been invited. There was to be a red carpet laid from the church to the road.

'And all the nobs in the district will be there,' Grandfather informed us as he went off to hoe the onions.

''Twill be a regular sight,' said Granny, 'a regular do. Shouldn't wonder if there isn't a thousand in the church.'

For days there was a mood of excitement in the district. It was as if there was going to be a Coronation or a Jubilee. Everyone talked only of 'the wedding'.

It was a fine day with summer shadows and summer lights. There were flowers and birds and small clouds drifting. The whole village poured out to watch. Crowds lined the path to the church. Crowds gathered among the tombstones and overflowed into the meadows beyond.

We stood in the garden of one of Aunt Georgie's friends and had a clear view, right to the church door. Soon after we'd settled, we heard the surge of the organ. Then the bells started, alerting everyone. All eyes watched the door.

Suddenly, out they came. The bride was like an angel, gliding along the red carpet with her white veil drifting round her like mist. Aunt Georgie dabbed her eyes and sniffed. She blew her nose and Mother made sentimental remarks about the day when she would watch *her* daughters emerge as brides from the village church.

Confetti filled the air. There were rose petals and rice. A car drew up for the bride and bridegroom. They climbed in, showered with good luck. Other guests departed in cars and it was all over. There was nothing left but confetti among the tombstones.

'That's it,' said Mother, breaking into the anti-climax with one of her terminating remarks.

'So now we'll all go home and have a nice cup of tea,' said Aunt Georgie and blew her nose again.

As we walked slowly back up the hill I felt depressed. I knew we'd never see the most important part of the occasion, that we had witnessed only the passing vision of a parade that would be most colourful and most exciting somewhere else. I couldn't bring myself to join in my sisters' excited conversation about the bride's dress and her bouquet.

Mother had said the wedding guests would now be having champagne, and though I'd never tasted champagne or ever seen any in my life, I knew it was rich and desirable, the liquor of gods and kings. I craved for it simply because it was rich and I wondered if I would ever manage to drink the cup of milk Granny would have ready when we got back.

'What did the bride look like?' Granny wanted to know as soon as we got in.

'Oh, a real picture, Mum. All in white from head to foot. With a veil what'd reach from here to Midhurst. And pageboys and bridesmaids and all. Ever so sweet they were, walking along behind her. There's never been a wedding to touch it in the village in my time.'

'She's a bit of all right, that gal, I reckon,' said Grandfather. 'Make a regular smart little wife, she will, I shouldn't wonder. Gals like that don't come two a penny, you know.'

'Many there?' asked Granny.

'Any God's amount,' said Aunt Georgie. 'All the village so far as I could see.'

'Except me,' said Grandfather, 'and *I* wasn't there. I got summat else to do, besides gaping at village weddings.'

5

Mother was a large woman with short brown wavy hair and soft, plump, sloping shoulders. She had thick legs, with wide calves which reminded me of the legs of a grand piano. They tapered to narrow ankles and small, slender feet. Father said she was fat, but she insisted that she was merely outsize.

'Big-boned,' she said, 'all my family are big-boned. And we all tend to put it on round the hips. But I'm not fat. No one could call me fat.'

Father did not argue and Mother didn't worry.

'In any case,' she went on, 'I really don't care what I look like. It's the way I feel that matters to me.'

She went about, winter and summer, with the sleeves of her dress pushed high above her elbows and her face glowing with warmth and health.

She made me feel smaller, thinner and paler than I really was, and I was often deeply ashamed of my cold hands and feet and icy, dripping nose.

'**One thing** is quite certain, dear,' she told me, 'you don't take after *me*!'

And then she predicted that I'd turn the corner when I was fourteen. It was a cheerful prospect but it seemed a long time to wait.

Most of the time, Mother was placid. It seemed impossible to rouse her from her easy-going attitudes and common-sense philosophies. When things were going wrong, she shrugged her shoulders and remarked that everything could be a great deal worse.

She often said 'What is to be, will be' and 'It'll all come out in the wash . . .' She reminded us continually that it was worse where there was none, and that it was 'colder without', and that a great many people were in far worse situations. I knew it was all true, but I never found any of it encouraging or comforting.

From time to time, however, something or someone did upset her. Then her whole personality was transformed. All the philosophies flew out of the window. Her grey eyes smouldered and turned dark blue.

In the days when we had an oil-burning stove for cooking, the wicks sometimes flared in a draught and set fire to the grease spilt round the burners. It scorched the washing airing on the line above. Yellow flames leapt to the ceiling, threatening the whole house. Mother's composure vanished. She rushed at the blaze, ordering everyone and swiping wet towels about, finding out with skilful detection just who had been responsible for leaving the back door open.

She was impatient with door-to-door salesmen and set tramps scuttling for the lane with her particular way of saying '*Not* today, thank you' which stopped all argument and sales talk. Next door, Aunt Georgie and Granny were not as successful. They listened to the hard-luck stories that sold the brooms and dusters, the daffodils and artificial flowers.

'Poor chap, he was in a bad way,' said Aunt Georgie. 'Got I don't know how many poor little children and a sick wife . . .'

'They all have,' said Mother, 'but he didn't fool me. He won't come bothering me again.'

The day a man came to the door selling religious tracts she really let herself go. It was just after breakfast and she was on her knees scrubbing the floor. My sisters and I were all on chairs, forbidden to move until the floor was absolutely dry.

'Who's *that* at this hour in the morning,' said Mother, scrambling up and heading for the door.

'No *thank* you,' we heard her say. She was more definite

47

than usual. 'I never buy tracts. I'm not interested in them. I have my Bible.'

'Most people have Bibles, but they don't read them,' said the man.

'*I* do not happen to be one of them,' said Mother crisply.

'Reading the Good Book is not enough,' he went on, and I thought what a fool he was to argue with Mother.

'It isn't easy to understand its teaching. The layman is not fitted to comprehend its great message. That is why I am here. To explain to you some of the Great Mysteries. That is what my papers are about; to point out the only true way to Salvation!'

'Just a minute,' said Mother. There was an edge on her voice, and she spoke slowly. I knew her eyes were growing dark.

'Don't misunderstand me, Madam,' said the man quickly. 'I have come to give you good news. The news that you may be saved. You, your husband and all your little children . . . those dear, innocent little kiddies, conceived in sin . . .'

'How dare you!' cried Mother. 'How dare you make insinuations like that! Let me tell you that I was brought up on the teaching of the Bible. And I know a great deal more about it than you ever will. My children have been brought up on it too. I just will not tolerate total strangers coming to my house and telling me what I should believe at nine o'clock in the morning!'

'I am obliged to warn you that you'll be damned! You'll be damned. All of you . . . doomed to be thrown into the pit of fire and brimstone . . . doomed to the everlasting torments of Hell . . .'

Mother sniffed. 'We are all entitled to our opinions,' she said. 'And now you'd better go before I lose my temper.'

Marooned on our chairs we looked at one another and said nothing.

'And one more thing,' said Mother. 'Don't you go calling next door. Everybody's out. Except an old lady over eighty. And *she* won't be interested. Don't you dare go frightening her with your blood and thunder.'

She slammed the door and the house shuddered. We heard her snorting on the doormat. There was a scuffle of steps and she went swiftly up the hall, unbolted the front door and rushed out. We knew where she'd gone and heard her thudding through Granny's kitchen, towards the back door.

She reached it in time to answer the knock.

'I thought I told you not to come here!' she cried and I would have given anything to have seen the man's face at this confrontation.

'Call yourself a religious man! Going about frightening poor old ladies to death! Clear off, double quick, before I call the police . . .'

There was the sound of his footsteps on the pitchen, the slam of a door and then mother's steps, thudding through the cottage again.

When she returned, she was red in the face. Damp strands of her hair fell from the clip.

'The very idea!' she exploded as she got on with the scrubbing. 'Whatever will people get up to next! I've no objection to them selling tracts if they really believe in what they're doing. But *that* man! Only last week he was working for a bookmaker in North Street. He got the sack for sticking to the takings. Who's he, for goodness' sake, to go round telling ordinary God-fearing people they'll end up in fire and brimstone. He'll know all about that if he goes on the way he's going!'

Every year Mother produced a Nativity play to raise money for the church. The first was in the local village hall, but there was a string of requests from other villages, so it was presented in their halls and eventually in the

The nativity play

cottage hospital and the workhouse. For a week before Christmas we were on tour: a confusion of late nights, rushed meals and problems of halls that were too small, with only oil lighting and often pianos that no longer played.

I was always cast as the Angel Gabriel because I was tall and thin and had blonde hair which Mother thought was ideal for the part, and because I was hopeless on lines and the Angel Gabriel had nothing to say.

My sisters were the Three Wise Men. The other parts were taken by village children, selected by Mother with her flair for finding suitable shepherds, saints and kings. The Virgin Mary was always played by a plump, fair-haired child with blue eyes. I thought she was stupid, but according to Mother she was a boon, as she sat smiling at the crib with a naturally devout expression.

The dressing rooms of these various village halls were too small for anything but the storage of the W.I. china and by the time the props, the costumes and Mother were in, there was no room for the cast. So we jostled and crowded, smudged one another's make-up; knocked off beards and bosoms, stumbled over straw and protested that we felt sick, had a terrible pain and had forgotten our words.

Mother struggled and sighed, pinned and re-pinned our clothes and continually entreated us to be quiet. . . . the audience was ready and the curtain was going up at any second. People had come to watch a Nativity Play, not to listen to our back-stage complaints.

'Besides, you certainly haven't forgotten your words,' she said. 'You'll remember them all right when the time comes. And don't even think about feeling sick. It's only imagination. . . .'

She jolted us into recovery. Only the Virgin Mary remained queasy. She was pale and cold and her blue eyes were blurred. She'd already been sick before she arrived. Now she pleaded that she dare not lean over the crib.

'Then just fold your hands and *pray* over it,' sighed Mother.

There was an Elsan lavatory in our village hall. It was in the corner of a tiny cloakroom by the main entrance, and was banned to us. The bucket was always full because there had been a village row about who was responsible for emptying it after the last wedding reception.

Mother said: 'None of you are to go there! The play won't last for ever. . . . you should have thought of things like that before you left home . . .'

Then the pianist began to thump the opening carol. The whole hall thundered with music, dust, darkness and the terrible jitters that precede a play.

I always came on towards the end of the last scene. I waited in the wings and trembled. Even the lobes of my ears shivered. I was hot and cold and desolate. My long white sheet, hanging in huge flutes, was filled with icy draught. My feet were numb.

The prompter prodded me in the back:
'Go on, Gabriel. Your cue . . . go *on* . . .'

One year Mother was more than usually venturesome about the scenery. She thought it would be nice to go in for more reality and less symbolism. So we built a stable of birch poles from the common and thatched it. It looked marvellous against the blue stage curtains with silver paper stars, dangling from black thread pinned to the ceiling.

As I took my place in the final tableau, I felt myself to be the most important character in the whole play. The lights were on me. I dazzled with splendour. It was literally the moment of pride before a fall. . . .

There came a fearful crack from above. The main

support of the stable roof gave way and landed heavily on my head. My halo was forced over my ears, stars of a magnitude I had never imagined appeared before me.

The Virgin Mary, the Kings and Shepherds blurred. Everything swayed in a sea of pain.

I knew only that I must remain in position. The effect of the tableau now depended on my ability to support the stable roof with my head.

No one realized what had happened, not even Mother, who watched the curtains close and then heaved a great sigh of relief because it was all over for another year.

'Why are you still standing there, dear?' she asked. 'The play's over . . .'

Sometimes there were days when Mother seemed to live in a dream, as if she had never been anything but even-tempered, musing on the secret thoughts in her mind, with her grey eyes fixed on some far-off star that only she could see. Softer, gentler, more patient, she was beautiful. I longed to put my arms around her and tell her so.

In these moods of dreams, she told us fascinating stories about her mother's family: unconnected details about huge woodland estates and big houses. Curious half-finished anecdotes about Nell Gwynne, Bonnie Prince Charlie, lost fortunes, illegitimate heirs and a remote French Duchess. As a descendant, Mother seemed strangely out of place among the scorched stew-pots and piles of dirty washing.

I looked at her with awe and was delighted. Romance drifted about the house. These were unexpected links with long-ago, bringing visions of satin-clad figures into the steam and confusion of the kitchen.

'She was the favourite of a king,' Mother went on, and I was pleased to learn that our ancestor had been notorious.

53

There was a half-smile in Mother's eyes and she was even more beautiful. I was intrigued because she never seemed to be quite so beautiful at any other time. I wondered why. I thought perhaps it was the unusual light in her eyes because she had withdrawn into the imaginary world of elegance and riches.

I forgave her all the bad cooking and the terrible burnt offerings.

'Of course,' she said, 'you must *never* tell anyone what I've just been telling you. It's not the sort of thing to talk about.'

After recounting such romantic family talks, she became extremely particular about table manners for a time, fussing over setting the meals properly and getting out the soup spoons and damask table napkins which had been among her wedding presents. They looked out of place in the untidy, steamy kitchen and Father took a look at the table and asked who we were expecting.

She instructed us in the etiquette of Court and Garden Party.

'You never know *what* you may need to know in life,' she said. 'It's better to learn while you're still young. You can always forget afterwards if you don't need the knowledge. But it isn't so easy to learn when you are older and suddenly need to know something special.'

When she had one of these moods, she spent a lot of time in her bedroom, going through drawers, taking out her collection of treasures as if they helped to confirm the dreams of that long past world. Laying them gently on the bed, she called us to come and see them.

Lovingly, she handled the silver-backed hair brushes, the ivory dressing sets and the delicate fans, the lace handkerchiefs and the mother-of-pearl card cases. She held up the family christening robe and said:

'Look at the size of the sleeves! No baby today would get a finger into that tiny opening, let alone its whole arm! The babies in those days were very small, you know.'

She picked up a porcelain bowl in which various delicate members of the family had been christened. She said it might have been priceless. But it was cracked.

'And that's a blessing,' she said, 'because it helps with the death duties. You have to pay death duties on everything you possess these days, you know . . .'

There was a box of lace mittens, oddments of ribbon, letters in a hand which ran across the page in thin, brown, almost unreadable scrawl.

'Listen to this!' said Mother and she picked up a faded letter and read it to us:

Dearest Mama,
I trust you are well. I am progressing with my studies. I

The wax doll

am anticipating the Easter Vacation when it will be my pleasure to see you. My health is good.
    I remain your most dutiful daughter,
        Ann Jackson.

'She was ten years old when she wrote that,' said Mother. 'She was my Great-great-grandmother.'

Finally, there was the doll with the wax face and arms.

'Don't touch her,' whispered Mother. 'Whatever you do, don't touch her!'

I didn't want to. She reminded me of a little corpse, lying there on the bed, staring at the ceiling with her pale, ice-blue eyes.

Long cloth legs dangled from her hips, and from the layers of petticoats and skirts tiny, fat feet protruded. They were stuffed into black satin slippers edged with pink ribbon and she wore delicate lace socks which had turned brown with age.

'She belonged to Ann Jackson, and I suppose she must have bitten off the tip of her nose . . .'

And the fingers were missing too. The hands lay like mutilated stumps on the bedcover.

The tangy odours of moth-balls and the strange, sweet scent of age breathed from the ancient creature.

'You've seen enough of her,' said Mother presently and lifted her tenderly and placed her in a cloth, the shroud of her safe-keeping, then carried her back to the drawer where she was laid among the vests and handkerchiefs.

These periods of disconnected romance and the displaying of the relics always disturbed me. There was a new mood of dignity in the house and I lay awake at night thinking. I saw bruised faces of waxen dolls staring into my dreams, and lace fans, opening and closing across the moon.

6

The river flowed in a dark, clay-brown stream near the village, slow-moving and cold, noisy only where the stony shallows rose from the bed. There were alders lining the banks, as dark and green as the water, casting deeper shadows and creating an avenue which seemed to lead into endless distances.

There were a stone bridge and a water-mill, and here and there beneath the alders, where the trees had thinned and the water swept in a great half-circle, there was sand, in great, heaped-up deposits, sloping steeply into the water, down and down, as if heading for some bottomless place in the heart of the earth.

Each year, these sandy bars changed, for the river itself changed, altering in subtle ways, developing fresh eddies, abandoning old ones, wearing away the banks, gradually creating for itself a new course. The winter floods eroded the sand, swept it downstream and deposited it elsewhere, so each season there were new and different beaches, different pools in which to swim.

Each season, my sisters and I set out to search for the best ones and when the sun was hot we made for the water and plunged in, splashing through the reeds like hunting spaniels. We swam about till we ached with the cold, then threw ourselves into the soft, warm sand to dry and recover. It blotted up the water, coated our bodies and filled our ears. Flavoured with fish and the green, waving weeds, it dried in the sun and brushed off our skin like pollen.

Idle and burning after the cold, we lay listening to the bees in the plants beyond the beach, watching the water voles along their narrow, water-side paths through the wet roots of the alders.

Sometimes, there were fish, leaping into the sunlight, tiny cutlets of silver, visible for an instant then back into the water with a splash and a gulp. It was impossible to see them as they swam in the stream, slow, invisible in the flickering reflections, moving secretly along with the current.

The riverside was often disturbed by cows coming to drink. They ploughed through the sand, their joints creaking and great barrel bodies swinging between small, stump legs. They dropped dung in great liquid green stars which spoiled the sand and filled the air with a sweet, grass smell. Into the water, they stood in a steaming crowd, flicking each other's noses with their tails. For a long time after they'd gone back to their pasture it was not possible to swim. The river was clouded and there was dung flowing to the reeds.

At other times we were disturbed by the village boys who came down to swim. Scorning all girls and aching with power and aggression, they took over the beach, the river and the fields beyond. Infuriated but powerless, we retreated, sometimes to another beach, sometimes to a hedge to wait for them to go.

They scuffed and punched one another, leapt about in the quiet pools and caused great tides to sweep over the sand. Then they stood in a row on the highest bank and peed into the water, competing for who could do the farthest. The whole place was a chaos of noise, splashing water, swirling sand and bodies. But when they went, we returned, smoothed the sand and slipped back into the water to swim again, as quiet as fish and cool as leaves.

Occasionally, we went to the sea. The nearest beach was only sixteen miles away, but the bus fares were expensive and Mother said there were too many of us.

It was only when Father had a car that we were able to

The bathing pool

go. He had a succession of them which were bought to
convert into vans for use in the business. But first, he took
us all out. Motoring was marvellous in the summer. We
seemed to sail through the countryside in fine style,
speeding along in warm breeze and yellow light. Blue
shadows raced past us. The soft creamy air flowed in and

59

lifted our hair. The wind sang and the road whisked beneath us in a ribbon of grey.

In winter it was different. It was terrible. Cars had no heating then and we were loaded with extra clothes. We also wrapped ourselves in blankets and huddled together, seeking any shelter going. The wind whistled through holes in the canvas hood and round the flapping side-screens. Bitter air worked through the rugs and pierced our legs and gnawed at our knees. The countryside was a colourless streak, hissing with cold, brittle with dead sticks and grass. Our noses dripped and we were too numb to do anything about it. We just sat waiting for the journey to end.

All these cars had dickey seats; they were ideal for conversion. It was simple to fix something on to the back in place of a seat. Liable to break down at any moment, they all hissed or trembled. They crept along the almost deserted roads at twenty miles an hour, with steam blowing out or with the engine sobbing hysterically.

We didn't care. Why should we? We knew nothing about cars or engines. All we understood was that it was marvellous to own a car at all, even if we knew we couldn't keep it for long.

Usually, the conversions went ahead as planned, but things could happen to a vehicle long before there was any work done on it, and sometimes Father got a good offer for it and he sold it, intending to get something better and bigger.

'The car's going Monday,' he would say. 'If you folks want to go anywhere, we'll have to go this Saturday. After Saturday it'll be too late.'

'Chichester!' Mother always said at once, and to Chichester we always seemed to go.

My sisters were crammed into the dickey seat and strapped in. I sat on Mother's lap in front and Father inserted the starting handle.

From then on, nothing went right. There was a rattle and a sudden shudder and the car seemed to vomit.

Father plunged up and down in front of the radiator, spat on his hands, wiped his face, blew his nose, spat on his hands again and had another go.

'Bloody thing . . .' he said and walked off. He disappeared for what seemed ages, but came back looking cooler and stood staring at the car, sucking his teeth and scratching his ears.

'Bloody thing,' he said again, less vehemently.

'I suppose you remembered to switch the engine on?' asked Mother. She only knew about this because of a previous occasion. 'And is there enough petrol in the tank? Of course, if you'd rather not go . . .'

'Oh for Chrissakes. . . .' said Father.

The engine eventually choked into life, the car trembled and, with the wheels grinding into the gravel at the roadside, we set off. After a few miles, we had to stop. A rattle had developed. Father was convinced the steering was going. He blamed us for fidgeting and said he could smell burning rubber and smoke. He leapt out, lay on his back and stared at the underparts of the car.

It was all very mysterious and upsetting and the gravity of the situation increased when he crawled out and announced that we wouldn't get any farther than the next cross roads. The only thing to do was to turn round and go home . . . unless we preferred to risk a journey with the certainty of a breakdown.

'And then we'll all have to walk home!' he said.

He didn't know why he ever suggested coming out at all. He said he was a bloody fool. The car was no good to anyone and never would be and buying second-hand cars was a mug's game.

Despite his prediction and the possibility of spending the night under a hedge, we continued the trip. The smell

61

of burning disappeared and suddenly there was no more knocking. The car began to skim over the road like a bird. And we reached Chichester.

Father always drove with immense concentration. He studied the road and gripped the steering wheel hard. His eyes, in the shadow beneath his hat, glinted with determination.

Our first car was a red three-wheeler, like a triangular biscuit tin. It had a black canvas hood and the side-screens had lost the studs which fastened them firmly. There was a triangular well in the pointed stem of this car into which my three sisters were fitted, one in each angle of the triangle. Mother sat in the passenger seat and I was wedged on her lap with my head against the hood and my legs jammed against the dashboard.

Father complained that the car was unbalanced. It would tip over and we'd all be killed. We didn't stand a chance, he said: over we'd all go at the first corner and that would be it. He put bricks under his seat to achieve balance and we set off with him complaining that the car was over-loaded and the tyres couldn't stand the weight . . . there wasn't a spare one, he hadn't got a jack or a puncture outfit and why we were going out at all only a fool knew.

'I ought to be certified,' he muttered.

'I'll light you a cigarette,' Mother offered, and to me she said: 'Duck your head, dear, I don't want to set fire to your hair.'

We had a square car next. There was more room, and according to Father it had greater potential for conversion. He said it was a nice little job and much more reliable.

Inevitably, Mother wanted to go to Chichester and we set off, sailing along the road as if we were driven by the wind. On the way home, Father said he thought we might run out of petrol if he wasn't careful. It would be a good thing to take a short cut over the downs.

'We can coast down the hill and save some,' he said.

As we swept over the crest of the steepest slope, he discovered that the brakes wouldn't work.

'Christ!' he gasped.

We headed into the valley at a speed unequalled by any car we'd ever possessed. The road plunged in a perpendicular ribbon. Far below, the village was a scattering of minute buildings. The wind screamed through the holes in the canvas. The hedges were a blur of blue and grey.

Mother clutched me and Father just kept on saying: 'Christ! Oh Christ. . . . Oh, Christ!'

The amazing thing was, nothing happened. Suddenly everything was over. We were gliding into Singleton, the village which had seemed so minute from the top of the hill. We swerved safely round the corners, over the bridge by the pub, and headed smoothly towards the hill which led out of the village; and all the way we had the whole road to ourselves.

'Christ!' said Father again. 'What the hell would have happened to us if there had been anything coming?'

'It's pointless to worry what might have happened,' Mother said.

'We might have all been dead under a bus,' he persisted.

'We might have been, but we aren't . . .'

Mother began to look at the view. Whatever she was feeling, she gave nothing away. But when we got back, she warned us to say absolutely nothing to Granny.

'You'll frighten the daylight out of her,' she said, 'and she'll never have a moment's peace when we're out.'

'As far as I'm concerned, we aren't likely to be going out again,' said Father. He dropped to his knees and crawled under the car.

But we did. Though it was some time later, because Father sold that car and it was a long while before he bought another. The new one was grey and we went off to spend a Bank Holiday by the sea.

On the way home, crawling through the Chichester traffic, the radiator began to boil. Steam rose like volcanic smoke.

'Do you want us to get out?' asked Mother.

'No,' said Father. He leapt out and dived into the steam.

The traffic halted behind us. Passing motorists asked when the tea was ready. Father grew red and his ears turned purple. Mother just sat and said nothing. She told us to keep quiet and to sit still because everything would be all right soon.

But it seemed ages, with us filling the whole town with steam and confusion. Then, miraculously, Father was back in the driving seat, pushing at the gears and we moved off. The rest of the traffic overtook us and everyone turned to look at the cause of the hold-up. I wished I was dead.

None of us spoke on the way home, for I suppose we all knew we were having our last trip out in a motor car for many, many years. Father's decision to finish for ever with family outings had got through to us. I was sorry. Despite the inconvenience and the minor disasters, there was something marvellous about travelling about in our own vehicle, and I was sad that we wouldn't be able to go again to the sea.

Sea-bathing was so much better than swimming in the river. Blue and gold, dazzling with gulls and sunshine, the wind smelled of shells and salt. The water was warmer and there were no cow-droppings clouding the pools by the groynes.

'We'll go to the sea tomorrow if it's fine,' Mother always said when one of these trips had been planned. She got up early to cut sandwiches.

She sat at the kitchen table, sawing away at the loaves,

slicing them into slabs. She scraped them with margarine and spread them with fish paste. She made flasks of sweet tea and filled bottles with lemonade. Aunt Georgie and Granny contributed extra milk, pots of jam and bags of biscuits because they were afraid we wouldn't have enough to eat.

While at the table, Mother ordered the rest of us to find baskets, sweaters, sandals, to fetch her knitting, the newspapers, her sun hat, cushions, rugs and peppermints; a lump of soda in case of stings and a bottle of calamine lotion for sunburn.

'And put my bathing costume in as well,' said Father one day.

'If I can lay my hands on it,' said Mother, 'but I've no idea where it can be. I'll have a look when I go upstairs later on.'

'If I know anything about it, it'll be under a ton of junk, half eaten by spiders and covered with dust.'

Mother said nothing.

This bathing costume of Father's was old-fashioned even in those days. Black and limp and faded to green and pale mauve in parts, it had wide shoulder straps, a high neck and long legs which reached half way down his thighs. The hems of the legs had stretched and become frilly at the ends.

I was so ashamed of this terrible garment I hoped the weather would turn cold so he wouldn't want to swim. No one ever wore such bathing suits any more and I wondered how on earth he could bear to put it on. No other man I knew would be seen dead in it.

Mother once suggested that it should be thrown away, or cut up for floor rags. She offered to knit him an up-to-date one. But he hadn't much opinion of her knitting.

'And the minute I get into the water, it'll stretch to glory and a nice sight I'd look with my costume round my ankles and me, stark, bloody naked! No, you leave it alone. I know it's all right as it is. It won't stretch any more than it's done already. And in any case, what's the matter with it? It's plenty good enough for me. My swimming days are pretty well over and done with. I'm not as young as I used to be and the water's not as warm, either.'

In spite of my desperate prayers, the day was fine and hot. The costume was fished out of the bottom of the wardrobe where Mother knew it was packed with everything else.

'It's riddled with moth,' she hinted.

'You don't need to tell me that. It's had moth holes as long as I can remember.'

'You let me have it when we get back and I'll darn it,' Mother promised. But he wouldn't hear of that.

'Don't waste any time on it,' he said, and he told her he'd decided to use it for straining paint. All he wanted was to wear it for one last dip.

Later, I watched, burning with shame, as he ran, stiff-legged, pale as a light-starved plant, working his arms like an athlete, towards the sea. The legs of the terrible suit flapped about him and the moth holes showed up in the sun in gleaming white spots. I felt everyone must be watching him and knowing he belonged to us. Then he plunged into the water and for a time the humiliation ceased. Relief flowed over me like warm milk. But if one focus of attention had gone, another quickly took its place.

As Father had waded into the water, the dog, which had sat patiently tied to his deck chair, began to bark.

'Oh, be quiet,' Mother ordered.

She was knitting and watching the sea. The dog gazed at her with reproach then barked again.

'Shut up!' said Mother. She snatched up a towel and flicked it at him. 'Can't you see, he's only gone for a swim?'

The dog gave her another look, then, before we realized what he was going to do, bolted towards the water, dragging the chair, the newspapers, Mother's ball of wool, Father's clothes, and a bag of sandwiches with him.

At that moment, someone who had been aiming pebbles at a spade stuck in a sandcastle, misjudged and hit me on the ear. The blow was sharp and scorching. My eyes filled with tears and for painful seconds, I saw the whole world tremble.

The sea heaved in a distorted haze. The crowds, the sand and the gulls flowed into it and everything turned green. When my vision cleared, I saw my father emerging from the water, looking like a thin, black seal. The costume clung to his body. The furrowed fabric lay in parallels across his stomach. Water dripped from the frilled legs like silver beads. The dog and the chair leapt about at his side in absurd welcome.

While he dressed, Mother put everything to rights. She sent my sisters and me to swim. When we came out we had the fish paste sandwiches, which were gritty after being turned out into the sand. Granny's buns had filled with sand too, and the jam was flavoured with salt and seaweed. Wasps appeared, conjured out of the air by the sweet scent of it.

We all chewed and shivered and I felt my hair hanging like wet string round my shoulders, dripping icy drops onto my sunburn. The air sparkled with light and reflections. Gulls glided and kites soared. There was the moan of a speedboat, and all the far-away noises of seaside places.

The sea water gradually dried on our bodies and our skin tightened like parchment. Time seemed to halt, even though Mother's knitting needles clicked like the ticking of a clock. In due course Father settled to sleep. Covering his face with his newspaper he slumped in the deck chair and began to snore.

People began to notice. They stared at us, showing signs of irritation in their eyes.

'Shut up, Fred,' said Mother as she knitted.

But the snoring continued, louder, more persistent, in deep, fruity rumbles.

'Throw some sand at the paper, dear,' said Mother, not speaking to any one of us in particular.

'Eh? What! Who's that! What! . . . Where . . .'

Father emerged from the newspaper looking red and bewildered.

'Nothing,' said Mother. 'Your imagination. Go back to sleep . . .'

Later on, a newspaper seller came trudging over the shingle.

'A Terrible Tragedy!' he shouted. 'Another Terrible Tragedy!'

The news brought reality back into the hot, lazy day. Father woke up and sent me to join the throng buying a paper. With his hat tilted over his eyes he searched for the tragedy.

'Well, what's happened?' asked Mother, presently.

'Damned if I know . . .'

The newspaper rustled as he re-scanned the pages.

'I doubt if there was a tragedy. It's just a way of selling a paper,' said Mother. Her knitting needles moved faster.

'*Widow Kicked at Whist Drive* . . . that must be it,' said Father slowly.

'Well, it may be,' said Mother. 'You couldn't call it comedy . . .'

She went on knitting, and far, far along the beach the man was still tramping on, shouting 'Another Terrible Tragedy', and selling his papers fast.

'He does it every day,' said a man near us. 'I buy his papers, but only because I want to know what won the two-thirty!'

'That's what I want to know,' said Father.

They got talking and then Mother and his wife exchanged domestic information and, inevitably, began to discuss children.

'Fine little girls you have there,' said the woman, looking at us, sitting in the sand eating biscuits.

'Yours are fine too,' said Mother.

'Never a day's illness . . .'

'Mine are never ill, either.'

'It's one of the great blessings of life, I say, healthy kiddies. And they don't quarrel, either.'

'Neither do mine,' said Mother. She was knitting fast and I sensed the competition.

'They never argue, either,' said the woman pleasantly. 'But then, I wouldn't expect them to. They're identical twins!'

There was a pause. The mood of triumph hung in the air for a moment, then Mother went into her grand finale.

'Mine are triplets,' she said, 'absolutely identical in every way. They even think alike.'

Father joined in the conversation, and recalled the famous achievement, that we'd all four been born in eleven months.

'Can't beat that one, can you?' he said with a grin.

The battle was won and everyone laughed. Then the tide began to turn and people began to pack up and leave the beach.

'We'd better go,' said Mother, winding in her wool. 'Once the tide starts coming in, it comes in fast.'

It was already licking at the sandcastles and erasing the cricket pitches. We rushed about, gathering shells, and found a strip of seaweed for Granny . . . she always liked to have a piece to hang by the back door where she could feel if it was damp or dry. If dry, she knew the weather was fine: if damp, she knew the weather was bad.

When we were back home again, she was pleased with

it. It was just what she'd been wanting, she said. Then she wanted to know what we'd been doing, and whether we'd been to Bognor or Wittering, and Aunt Georgie made us hot milk and said she'd been worried all day, in case one of us went too far out and got drowned.

'And that old car,' said Granny, 'I did wonder about that. Will said as the big end wasn't any too good.'

In bed in the darkness I could still hear the surge of the waves in my ears. My shoulders burned and there was sand in the sheets.

In my dreams the paperman marched about, shouting 'Another Terrible Tragedy! Another Terrible Tragedy!'

Then the tide swept over me and there was no more.

7

My greatest ambition was to become Curator of the British Museum. I asked my mother if she thought there was any chance for me. She was washing up and didn't even look up from the sink.

'No, dear,' she said, 'I shouldn't think so for a moment.'

But she suggested that it might be a good idea to start a museum of my own if I really wanted to run one.

'It's easy,' she said. 'All you have to do is to find some relics and things. Anyone can find the skeleton of a Brontosaurus if they look in the right place. You stand as much chance as anyone.'

She convinced me that the world was a potential treasure ground, bulging with relics, all lying around, ready to be unearthed: skeletons of mammoths in Grandfather's garden, the remains of prehistoric man beneath the heather all over the common and the foundations of Roman palaces under the cabbage patch beyond the privy. The whole world, it seemed, was my archaeological oyster. But after the first, mad dream I ceased to believe in the presence of locally submerged skeletons and turned to smaller, easily acquired relics just waiting to be picked up—the fossils in the flint stones on the common, birds' feathers dropped in the grass, dead beetles and discarded birds' nests in the hedges.

My sisters caught the enthusiasm and we concentrated on collections until our bedroom was crammed. We balanced the birds' nests on the dressing-table and along the window-sill. The fossils were arranged on the mantelpiece and chest of drawers. We hung twigs from pictures and pinned dead beetles and moths to sheets of paper hanging on the back of the door, on the curtains, and over the wardrobe mirror.

71

Museum in our bedroom

Once it was known that we were running a museum, a supply of treasures poured in. Everybody saw the opportunity to get rid of all the junk they didn't actually want, but couldn't bring themselves to throw away. We were showered with the sentimental souvenirs of fishing trips, collections of birds' eggs made by long-grown-up sons and the colourless, pressed flowers from forgotten holidays. There were cases of moths, lumps of unidentified rock, jugs, mugs, pipes and postcards.

The greatest source of our supply was Mrs Wells, one of Aunt Georgie's friends. She attended all the local sales and jumble sales and acquired things she didn't want; all the oddments that were thrown in with something else . . . dozens of things that were absolutely useless and suitable only for filling the shelves of a museum.

She gave us a case of stuffed fish; two pike which she said had been caught in the mill pool by her grandfather. Huge green, varnished monsters, suspended in the fictitious world of their glass case, they snarled eternally towards each other's tails.

Mrs Wells told us the river was filled with pike. They lurked under the roots of trees in the deep, dark pools and she hoped we were very careful when we went bathing in the river, or we'd get attacked and probably bitten to death. She also gave us a case of stuffed birds; blackbirds, redwings and various finch, all perched among the weird tufts in a faded, papier-mâché landscape. We perched these cases on top of the chest of drawers and Mother looked on with controlled exasperation and asked us not to scratch the ceiling.

Mrs Wells also gave us a huge lump of coral, a zither, an eighteenth-century harvest bottle and a Grecian vase – at least, she said it was a Greek one. It was shaped like the body of a cow. The rim was chipped and there had been a pair of hands clasping the neck. It was difficult to make out what had originally been there. Mrs Wells thought it was a nymph, because the side of the vase was decorated with figures in bas-relief, all prancing and dancing and reclining in curious postures. The figures were naked and had round prominent buttocks which reminded me of cherry stones.

Mrs Wells said the figures depicted Apollo sporting with the Maidens.

'But really, I don't know *what* they are supposed to be doing . . .' she said carefully.

We took the vase home at once and showed it first to Aunt Georgie. She was picking peas and her face was hot and pink and turned even pinker when she saw the vase.

'Really me! Wherever did you get that from! My, my! What *will* they decorate vases with next!'

Mother was impressed, but told us to take it upstairs at once because the butcher was due any moment.

'I wouldn't show it around too much,' she said later. 'It may be very valuable, and it's better not to publish your valuables too freely.'

Our museum caused a certain amount of family interest. Father, of course, made fun of it. He said the fossils would be useful for concrete and what good were fish unless you could eat them? Granny was worried because it was all kept in the bedroom. She was convinced that we'd catch something from the relics.

'All they dead birds and maggits!' she cried. 'All up in the room where they little gals sleeps! It ent right, reely it ent. You shouldn't allow it, Ivy. You don't know where some of they old relics have bin!'

Aunt Georgie wasn't easy about the museum, either. She worried about germs, too, and was nervous of the snake skins. She was absolutely terrified of snakes and suffered agonies of doubt when we discovered a sloughed-off skin on the common.

'Leave it alone, for Lord's sakes!' she cried as we eased the fragile, scaly thing from the heather.

'Oh my Lord!' she screamed. 'And now you've bin and put your hands to your faces. . . . Oh, whatever will you do next!'

Her worst agonies were caused by the owls' pellets lying under the trees by the warren path.

'It's dog's dirt!' she gasped. 'Put it down at once! Throw it away as far as you can see. Oh, the nasty, messy stuff! Oh my Lord, whatever will you children pick up next!'

She paced the sandy track, flinging her hands about helplessly. We argued coolly, informing her that the pellets ejected by owls consisted of undigested food, bits of bone, wing cases of beetles and the teeth of mice.

We pulled them to bits to show her, but she wouldn't even look.

'I don't want to see!' she cried. 'I'm not interested, and I'm going off home at once. I won't go another step if you will persist in playing about with dog dirt!'

We grew bored with the museum. Dust settled on the fossils and there were cobwebs in the decaying nests. The wings of the moths faded and nothing seemed valuable any more. We cleared everything away, tossed the stones into the garden and put the zither in the roof. The Grecian vase broke as we carried it to the garden shed.

The bedroom suddenly looked huge and empty. The pink roses on the wallpaper seemed to bloom and there were echoes in the empty corners.

Mother told Aunt Georgie: 'It's just as I said it would be. They'd get fed up with it. It's always the same with children. Let them do what they want and they don't want to do it. But try to stop them and they just get more determined. Now I can get some new curtains. And I'll get Fred to paint the window . . .'

As the collecting interest waned, we became concerned with living things instead.

There were so many birds about. The garden was

haunted by finches, tits, starlings, thrushes and black-birds. There were snipe, plovers and curlews on the common; meadow pipits, yellow buntings, stonechats, willow warblers and chiffchaffs on the hills. In the copses there were long-tailed tits, wrynecks and blackcaps. There were kingfishers by the river; sedge warblers, moorhens, coot and dabchicks by the ponds.

All the thickets in the village seemed to be filled with nightingales. There was a pair in the sandpit, just behind our two cottages. Others were in the thicket at the cross-roads. They haunted every bush in the lane. The spring nights were filled with song.

Everyone looked forward to their coming and the first song of the year was news. Everyone told everyone else they'd heard the nightingale . . . but later, as the songs went on, throbbing monotonously into the night and through most of the day, people began to complain.

'You don't get a chance to sleep . . . singing away, fit to bust, all night and all day . . . you'd think they'd want a bit of rest sometime, wouldn't you?' Grandfather asked Mrs Wells.

'Nightingales sing in their sleep, Mr Budd,' she said.

She and Grandfather were sitting on the garden seat, discussing the news and the spring.

'I near as dammit chucked my boots at 'em last night, I did,' Grandfather told her, 'not that it would have done much good, I don't reckon. Nothing upsets 'em when they be wound up. Sing through any old row when they've set their mind to it. You wants to hear 'em in a storm. They goes at it fit to bust in a thunderstorm. The louder the thunder rolls the louder they birds sings!'

'We got some in the thickets behind our woodshed,' said Mrs Wells. 'A regular concert up there, there is. Night after night. My Bert sticks corks in his ears. He can't sleep no sense, else.'

Early in the spring the lapwings came to the common.

76

Suddenly they arrived and were swooping in the sky, swerving over the bog and crying plaintively and endlessly.

The sound of them seemed to bring in the scent of the sweet black mud and the pale sphagnum moss. It was a wild, lonely sound and I went out to search the bog for their nests.

As I plodded among the tufts of sedge, the birds hurled themselves about me, mobbing me because I was interfering. Their eggs were laid in the grass. They were a beautiful mud-brown, speckled with black, so perfectly camouflaged, they were difficult to see.

I found a newly hatched chick, crouching in the whiskers of the dead grass, covered with down, as fragile as a wisp of thistledown. As I bent over it, the parents swooped in an agony of protest. One dropped into the bog beside me, a few feet from the chick. It began to limp as if it was wounded, dragging a twisted wing. It went into the grass, leading me over the mud, away from the chick and, as I followed, it recovered and with a flick of its feathers, shot into the air with a cry of triumph and swept easily into the wind like a fragment of charred paper.

There were six ponds on the common, each one in the dip of a valley with bracken growing thick on the slopes and stiff, yellow sedge fringing the water. Haunted by water-birds, they were filled with frogs, dragonflies, water-boatmen and the larvae of millions of pond creatures, which flew, skated, swam and dived.

The fascination of these deep-water treasures was irresistible. My sisters and I dredged the mud with jam jars tied to string. Wading, thigh-deep, into the soft mud at the pond's edge, we searched and waited, watching like fishermen. The mud gave off a strange, sweet scent and the water was cold as frost, even in the summer. In the early morning, pale scarves of mist lay on the water and there were voices of invisible birds in the reeds.

Catching newts

In due season, drifts of cotton sedge appeared in the surrounding bog like flakes of stranded snow. At their roots grew sundew, milkweed and sticky pink and crimson lousewort. From time to time there was the call of a curlew and the drumming of a snipe: cries that were strangely sad and remote, exclusive to these water-logged places and the lonely hills around them.

The best pond for hunting in was the one across the

road from our cottage. It was the largest and deepest of them all and considered to be the most dangerous. There was, they said, a huge and bottomless hole in the centre, and an unknown soldier had ridden into the pond to water his horse on a dark night and vanished.

The legend lingered, but had no foundation. No one really knew anything about it. Mother said it was one of those tales which lose nothing in the telling. But Granny believed every word of it. She was convinced that the hole was there, bottomless and dangerous, and she was wracked with fear whenever she knew we'd gone fishing.

'You'll all fall in and no one will ever see you again,' she warned. 'Where's the sense, messing about in dirty old ponds, catching yer deaths, that's what I wants to know.'

'I should be careful,' said Aunt Georgie, 'there may be broken glass . . . don't get too far out, that's all. You never know with old ponds. You just never know.'

'Bodies!' said Grandfather, sucking his pipe. 'They used to throw bodies in ponds in the old days. There was one in that pond up near Wispers. The keeper shot his gun acrost it and the body just come floating up, just like that.'

'O reely me,' said Granny, but she'd run out of words to express her feelings.

That pond was absolutely infested with creatures. They swarmed in the thick, fertile mud. There was caddis-fly larvae, the big, dark blue diving beetles, leeches which moved like pieces of wet brown elastic, scorpion-like dragonfly larvae and mosquito nymphs. The surface was alive with dancing flies, water-boatmen, skaters and oddments.

There were newts, too. Thousands upon thousands of newts. The easiest of all the pond creatures to catch, they crawled obligingly and almost instantly into every jar that was trailed before them. It seemed a good idea to

79

see how many it was possible to catch at a standing and
one early spring afternoon we took the big galvanized
kitchen bath to the pond and settled to fish.

One after another, out they came, these treasures of
the mud, and we soon lost count of them. Sometimes
there were two in the jar at a time, gazing through the
glass like mildly astonished fish. Then, the excitement of
the glut was over and with the pride of fishermen we
carried the great catch back in the bath to impress the
family.

'Good gracious!' said Mother, pausing in her knitting.
'I'd no idea there were *that* many newts in the world! Go
and get your Aunt Georgie. I'm sure she'd like to see them.'

But Aunt Georgie did not like to see them. She turned
pale at the sight of the mass of dark, slowly swimming
creatures.

'Oh!' she gasped. 'Oh! What *dreadful* little creatures!
Take them away . . . take them outside, for Lord's sakes.
They make me feel quite ill, they do. All squirming about
in the water like that!'

Granny pottered in, with a pucker of curiosity on her
face. She'd heard the exclamations.

'Newts, Gran,' said Mother. 'They've been catching
newts in Black Pond.'

'And there's millions of 'em! Just millions!' wailed
Aunt Georgie.

'Effetts?' asked Granny, with alarm. 'Effetts? Don't
you have effetts in the house, Ivy. Jump out and be all
over the place they will, before you know what you be at.
Jump into yer mouths they will if you give 'em half a
chance. Choke you to death if they get into yer stummicks
they will. Oh, take 'em away, do, for mercy's sakes.'

Mother went on knitting, calm and disbelieving.

'Crawled out of that great big hole, I shouldn't wonder,'
Granny continued fearfully. 'There must be thousands
of 'em, all living in that great, big hole.'

'Probably,' said Mother vaguely. She advised us to put them back in the pond.

'After all, you can't *keep* them,' she said, 'and they'll only die if you leave them in a crowd like that for long.'

'Yes, you take 'em back afore they starts jumping out on us all,' Granny said.

So we carried them back and there was a mood of anti-climax in the dusk as we unloaded them into the pond like a monster shoal of fish. In half a moment, they had all gone, vanished into the cloud of mud among the roots.

There were other pond creatures to capture, but they were elusive and hard to find, not gullible and easy, like the newts. They appeared occasionally in the jars, scuttling about in the sudden light around them, or clawing at the sides to get out.

The dragonfly nymphs were among these. Pale, mud-brown, scorpion like and sinister, they were like miniature dragons on the defensive. During the summer we found them on the stems of the reeds, far above the water, but empty and dry, brittle and transparent. The dragonflies had emerged, leaving the cases to blow away like dead leaves.

In a dip in the side of a dung heap I found a clutch of grass snake eggs. They were soft and shell-less, and lay like small oblong fungi in the muck.

I took them home and put them in a cardboard box with a piece of glass on top and spent the day on the watch, hoping to see them hatch. The eggs lay for two days and then a small dark head protruded from one of them. It flicked a minute, black tongue in and out and its eyes gleamed like the eyes of mice. By the afternoon, several heads had emerged and in the evening small black snakes were wriggling in the box. They were beautiful creatures, with pale blue undersides and a delicate grey sheen on their backs.

'*Please* don't keep them,' said Mother. 'We don't want snakes swarming all over the house, and if Granny knows you've got them she'll die of fright. In any case, it isn't right to keep wild creatures in captivity. They lose their ability to defend themselves as they should. Let them go.'

I took them out to the common and tipped them into the heather. Swiftly they wove like thin, black threads into the undergrowth and vanished. I was sorry. I'd had them for such a brief time and they had left me only their empty egg cases. I tossed these into the gorse and went home.

A few days later a creature like a monster wasp was clinging to the curtain in the kitchen.

Wide metallic wings were spread stiffly from an oblong body which had a brilliant orange end. On this was stuck a large spike about half an inch long.

I looked at it, and, for all my love of wild things, I froze with horror and then bolted.

'What on earth's the matter with you?' asked Mother.

'There's a creature in the kitchen,' I said.

'There are often creatures in our kitchen,' observed Mother.

'This one's got a sting a mile long. It's absolutely fearful. Orange and black, with huge wings.'

'Don't exaggerate, dear,' said Mother, but she went out to look for herself.

'There! On the curtain!' I said, creeping up behind her.

There was a second of dead silence as she saw it. Then she said.

'Yes . . . Well, yes. It *does* look rather ferocious. . . .'

'But what *is* it?' I demanded.

'I really don't know. You're the expert on these things.'

We went back to the sitting-room and Mother closed the door behind us. She got out the Insect Book.

'Things that *look* ferocious generally aren't,' she said philosophically as she flicked through the pages.

'This must be it. A female wood wasp . . . and the spike is an ovipositor . . . used for depositing eggs in the wood of conifers, where the grubs hatch out and feed. They burrow in the heart-wood for years. And it says the creature is absolutely harmless.

'There you are!' she said, snapping the book shut. 'You can pick it up and it won't hurt you at all!'

But nothing on earth would have persuaded me to touch it. I didn't even want to see it again.

Mother picked up her knitting.

The wood wasp on the curtain

'*I* think it's better to leave it alone and it'll fly out when it feels inclined. Just go and open the door and it can go as it wishes.'

There were butterflies in the garden all the summer, dipping into the flowers, dancing over the hot, dry grasses. The first one to appear was usually a brimstone, a solitary, lime-yellow creature, fluttering boldly into an early spring day, attracted by the sudden sunshine.

'A butterfly! I saw a butterfly!' we said and it was as marvellous as hearing the first cuckoo.

Later there came a stray tortoiseshell, a cabbage white, and finally, early in May, the orange tips. Our garden was haunted by orange tips, hundreds of them over the newly opened flowers. They were in the hedgerows, out in the meadows; nothing but orange tips until they were joined by the cabbage whites, and the little Clifden blues and the tortoiseshells.

Grandfather regarded the white ones with a sniff of disapproval.

'Laying eggs on my cabbage they be,' he said. 'Watch out for palmers in the dinner, George.'

The green and yellow caterpillars hatched quickly and all through the summer the cabbage needed special attention. Grandfather sometimes searched the plants and picked them off before they ate too many of the leaves.

'They gets through some cabbages, they palmers, and no mistake,' he said, 'but 'tis a job to see 'em. They looks so much like the leaves.'

Mother was bad at cleaning cabbages, always missing caterpillars, so they turned up, looking pale and limp, in the dinner and everyone but Father hid them under the rim of the plate or dropped them discreetly beneath the table.

Father liked to make a drama of a boiled caterpillar. He held it up on his fork.

'Look at that!' he said. 'Look at what I've got in my

84

dinner! Big as an eel. Make a meal in itself, it would!'

From then on, he searched his plate, warning everyone to do the same. You never knew, he said, *what* you'd find, if you didn't keep a sharp look-out.

In the late season, the red admirals and peacocks arrived and made straight for the buddleias. They spent their days obsessively among the long purple blossoms in the thick, sweet warmth of the September sunshine.

At night there were moths. They came quivering onto the window-sill, then into the room and began to fly madly round the lamp-glass. They stunned themselves and burned their wings and some of them died on the table below.

There were tigers, gorgeous red and gold creatures, with black and white spots. There were magpies, tussocks and puss-moths: and the pale fawn ones that were so numerous we never knew one from another.

There were also unknown ones, the rare ones that came to the window and hovered ponderously in the dark. Big as birds and impossible to lure to the lamp, they remained on the edge of the night and then vanished. None of us ever knew what kind they were and we did our best to impress each other by descriptions.

'It was as big as that!' we said, demonstrating like fishermen, and none of us would have argued that it was not.

Sometimes we kept caterpillars in glass jars on the dresser or the kitchen window-sill. Mother developed quite an interest in them and often abandoned the washing-up and the cooking to watch them feed.

Father observed the captives and said it wasn't enough to find them in the cabbage. 'We'd have them in the cake next . . .'

Some buried themselves and changed into dark capsules with jointed ends which writhed about at a touch. They remained in the earth all winter and hatched in the early summer. Hanging precariously to the dresser shelf, the newly emerged moths, still crumpled, soft and damp, quivered as they waited to expand their wings ready to fly off into the night. One of them once laid a batch of eggs. Mother was spring-cleaning the dresser and she discovered them, all over the shelves and china.

'I'll keep an eye on them,' she said. 'We'll put the little caterpillars in a box when they hatch.'

But they hatched unexpectedly. One morning we found the dresser swarming with minute black creatures. They crawled over the cups, in the salt, over the mustard and in the egg cups.

'I don't know *what* your father will say,' said Mother, and she gave him breakfast in bed and said nothing about it.

All day, she worked with a paint brush, lifting the minute things and dropping them into a box. At last she thought she'd got them all.

'But I really don't know,' she said. 'There may be some, still crawling about. But if any of you find one floating in your tea, for goodness' sake don't make a song about it. Just take it out and say nothing.'

Grandfather considered caterpillar-keeping an odd pastime.

'I spends all my time getting rid of 'em,' he said, 'and you gals looks after 'em as if they was gold dust.'

Amused, he sucked his pipe loudly.

'Now, if you'd go around collecting some of the blackfly on my beans, there'd be some sense. I never see the blackfly like it is on my beans this year!'

He got Aunt Georgie to save all the washing water and twice a day he went out and drenched the bean rows with it.

'Regular good stuff this is,' he told Granny as he worked the syringe.

'It smells terrible,' she said.

'I'd be surprised if it didn't,' he replied. 'Georgie's been washing my old socks in it. You couldn't have nothing better for the blackfly than what my old socks have bin washed in!'

8

Of all the spring mating ceremonies I watched, the pied wagtails' was the most frantic. Out on the lawn the cock dipped his head and spread his wings till they appeared like the petals of some extraordinary piebald flower, swirling against the grass. He drew them in and began to circle the hen until he was moving so fast he became a blur of grey.

A cock pheasant conducted his courtship with elegance, pacing the rough grass of the meadows beyond the garden. He presented himself with a flourish. It was a pity the hen was so indifferent. He was fat with the promise of love and gleamed with the passion of the spring. But she didn't seem to notice or care. She stared at the ground and crept into the grass, seeking food like an over-grown mouse peering at the moss.

Sparrows did their mating with little preparation. They performed agile, hovering visitations on the ridge tiles of the cottage. They proceeded to the gutters. Then did it all over again on the telephone wires. On and on, all through the summer they mated and nested, quarrelled and filled the roof with protesting young.

In the big oak tree opposite the builders' yard at the end of the garden path there were wood pigeons. Side by side, in the huge spreading branches, they settled and moved their little heads with soft creamy movements. Their courtship was long and tender. They crooned and purred, bowed and finally merged in a blur of feathers, flapping with bird-love. The pigeon romance went on all summer, too. Courting and mating, crooning and nesting, it seemed there was nothing else to interest them.

In April the nightingales settled in, nesting in the sandpit in the lane.

Grandfather said:

'They nightingales be going full bore again, Nell.'

Then came swallows and house martins, the cuckoos and, lastly, the turtle doves and nightjars.

The soft song of the doves was the final confirmation of the summer. Their voices were in every glade and hedge, in every green lane.

At night it was the purring of the nightjars. Their voices as monotonous as bees, soft as the doves, ferny, remote and lonely, they filled the night and in the patterns of the moonlit bracken they flitted soundlessly as shadows.

In every pipe lying in the builders' yard, in every crack in every wall, in every hole in every tree, there was a tit's nest. Blue tits, great tits, they were everywhere, and Grandfather wasn't pleased.

'Little buggers,' he said. 'After my peas at every opportunity they gets, and we lets 'em nest in the garden.'

Father went about chalking 'Tit's Nest. Keep Away' on bits of board which he propped against the nesting site. He wrote on the sides of the pipes and hung warnings on the apple trees.

A pair of blue tits always nested between two loose bricks over Granny's back door. Each year, when they arrived, Grandfather declared he'd stop up the hole when they'd hatched off and gone. Then, in the year to come they wouldn't be able to get in.

It wasn't that he minded them nesting there, he said, but it was all the worry they caused . . . all the fuss when the young birds hatched and dropped into the kitchen . . . and what with the cats trying to get them and everyone rushing about all day, shifting the furniture and hiding his boots, they were more nuisance than they were worth.

'Look after the little buggers all the summer, we do, then the minute they fly off, they go straight for my peas!'

89

He sniffed loudly and knocked his pipe on the heel of his boot.

The babies hatched in due course, and in due course the first one fell out of the nest and into the kitchen. Somehow it had managed to work its way down through the cracks in the plaster over the door.

Aunt Georgie rushed straight into our house for help. 'Quick!' she screamed. 'A baby bird! It's just bin and dropped onto the window-sill. Come quick before the cats get it. My hands are covered with flour and there's cats all over the place.'

We dropped everything and rushed to the rescue. The little bird was sitting on the ledge among the reels of thread, trays of pins, gloves, scarves and screwed handkerchiefs. It was huddled in a feathery ball, with its big, pale beak pointing towards the ceiling like an arrowhead. It was both ugly and beautiful and, I thought, looked incredibly old, like some withered Aztec idol.

We dived for the cats first, snatching them from their innocent sleep by the kitchen fire, and flung them, astonished and dopey, into the big room.

It was easy enough to capture that first fledgling. It made no attempt to fly. It made no struggle against capture. It was easy to push it gently back into the nest crack. But it wasn't long before the others sought freedom. Then, once they'd started, they fell out all day long. The parents fluttered about in a state of continual agitation. And in and out of the kitchen we raced, tossing cats, slamming doors, diving between the furniture.

At least once a year, one of the little birds got itself wedged behind the dresser. It worked its way farther and farther into the darkness and there was absolutely no way of getting it out without moving the whole dresser and its contents. Needless to say, the dresser was laden with a mountain of things that Aunt Georgie had been steadily building up throughout the winter months.

Fit for a Duchess

We knelt on the floor, flashing a torch, listening for sounds, trying to discover the position of the bird. Then, sooner or later, there came the faint movement of its claws, the rustle of a feather and long periods of silence.

'Now it's bin and died of fright!' said Aunt Georgie.

'I doubt it,' said Mother. 'Come along, we'll have to move the dresser away from the wall, then we can reach it.'

We unloaded everything. The whole vast collection of needlework, washing, Christmas presents, newspapers, plates, letters, chocolate, parish magazines and library books.

Granny hovered, getting in the way, and asking continually if it was going to be all right. She warned us to be careful not to tread on it and to mind the spiders and the pins.

Grandfather looked in to make further comments on fussing over a bird that would grow up and eat peas and then, only when the whole kitchen had been turned upside down and the dresser was visible for the first time in months, was it possible to ease it away from the wall.

The bird was invariably sitting on the ledge of the wainscot, dazed and draped with cobwebs and the wing-cases of dead beetles and the legs of bluebottles.

'Poor little thing!' said Aunt Georgie. 'Poor little mite! Look at its little eyes! Look at its little wings! Oh, the dear little thing! The poor little mite!'

On and on she crooned, while we plucked it out of the dust and pushed it back into the nest.

Then there was the kitchen to put into order. And with the bird out of the way, Aunt Georgie turned to the things that had fallen behind the dresser . . . things she had lost for months, things she didn't even remember she possessed.

'And look! There's Father's blue socks and his funeral tie!' she cried, descending on them in a swoop of glee. 'I've been looking all over the place for them! How on earth could they have got down behind the dresser? Oh, and there's the thimble . . . the one Mrs Jervis-Smith gave me . . . and Constance's letter. And just look at that mouse's nest! Did you ever see a mouse's nest behind the dresser before?'

'Meece?' cried Granny, alarmed. 'Did you say meece, George?'

It was a time of triumphant rediscovery and we all enjoyed it.

'I wish I could see what there is,' said Granny wistfully. 'I do miss seeing like I could in the old days.'

'It's just as well you can't, Mum,' said Aunt Georgie. 'You go and set down by the fire and keep out of the way, there's a dear.'

Grandfather looked in again, scanning everything without comment. Then he said:

'Looks to me we could do with a few more tom tits in the place.'

In the lane, just beyond the sandpit, there nested a pair of red-backed shrike. They haunted the briar thickets and blackthorn which were so dense that not a speck of light showed through. Like a huge compressed bird's nest, it had been building up for generations. No plant grew there, only moss and silver lichen on the dead, brittle twigs.

It was a perfect haunt for shrikes. Here they dwelt, skimming the thicket, perching on top of the tangle, bleating into the countryside with their weird goat-voices. They were beautiful, grey and white, brick red and black, with black bars over their eyes which made them look fierce.

Granny, pottering in the garden, often heard them and paused to listen.

'The Butcher Birds!' she said. 'They be back again, down in the old thick-set hedge.'

'They bin there since I was a boy,' said Grandfather.

The red-backed shrike

'There have always bin Butcher Birds in these parts.'

Late one spring we found a larder. It was a small branch laden with a store of carrion caught by the birds and impaled on the thorns for later eating. Mice, bluebottles, beetles, the tail of a lizard. The mouse was half eaten and the bit that remained smelled rotten. The bluebottles might have been fresh. They did not smell, but gleamed in the sun with the blue of sapphires and the green of emeralds.

Grandfather was impressed by our interest in wild birds.

'What they gals don't know about birds ent worth knowing,' he told the Sunday visitors.

Not knowing one bird from another, they said:

'Well, that's better than running after boys, isn't it?' and shrieked with laughter and winked.

But Mrs Hunt, who once came with some distant cousins of Grandfather's, was really impressed and when we told her there was a robin's nest in the lane, only a little way down the hill, she wanted to see it.

We took her out, my sisters and I, with pride. Gently we approached the nesting hole and for a second the bird gazed out through the surrounding leaves in consternation.

Then it flew off in a whirl of haste. Where it flew to, none of us knew. It simply vanished. But Mrs Hunt was convinced that it had flown straight up her skirts.

With a yelp of terror, she clutched herself. She flapped her skirt. She sprang into the road and began to scream.

Mrs Hunt and the robin's nest

94

Her fur jacket bristled. She kicked her legs like a distressed ballet dancer and fat, white thighs showed over the tops of her stockings. There were glimpses of lace, ribbon, and pink satin knickers.

'*Do* something!' she screamed. But we stood fascinated, so astonished at the display that we couldn't even laugh.

'Can't any of you *do* anything?' she pleaded. 'Where's that bird?'

She was furious and desperate. Then suddenly she started to cry.

'Where *has* that bird gone?' she wailed.

'Over the hedge,' we told her. But she didn't believe it and launched into another fit of panic.

There was a renewed exhibition of thighs and under-clothes and then, exhausted, she asked to be taken back to the house. She wanted to undress, to make absolutely certain, I suppose, that there was no bird caught in the hem of her petticoats or the frills of her french knickers.

The next visitor to be interested in birds was a far-removed cousin called Harold. He had come with his girl friend, Alice, to stay for a week and told us he was keen on nature.

'What I'd really like,' he said, 'would be to watch birds by the waterfall. I'd like Alice to see the waterfall and perhaps she'll work up an interest in nature.

'Are there any kingfishers at the waterfall?' he asked.

Mother thought that we should *all* go to the waterfall and she packed sandwiches and told us not to be too late getting back.

In the pool below the fall were islets of sandstone boulders which had fallen from the rock face. We chose the biggest for the picnic site and sprang from boulder to boulder to reach it. Beech trees grew from the banks above and leaned down towards the centre of the pool in a great, green canopy. Visible in the rock, the roots held loose boulders, preventing them tumbling into the pool. There were dark green ferns and moss among the stones, and the air was green and cool with the smell of mud and fish. The enduring splash of the water was accompanied by the whispers of the stream running away southward.

'Spooky,' said Alice, who had spent the morning getting herself up for the picnic. She didn't seem to like the island much and couldn't find a comfortable place to sit.

We had a hunch she wouldn't like it. She hadn't taken to the country at all. We knew Harold would never get her interested in Natural History.

'Where are the kingfishers?' she asked, looking wearily up at the trees.

'Oh, they'll come out when they've got used to us,' said Harold. 'They're most likely watching from some hole in the bank.'

'It's cold,' she said, rubbing her arms.

'Have my sweater, then,' said Harold.

'I don't want your sweater . . .'

She sniffed and looked miserable.

Harold looked miserable. She turned and stared at the pool.

'I know!' he said. 'Alice and I will sit and watch for the kingfishers, while you go upstream and drive them down to us.'

Anything was better than being marooned on a tiny island with Alice so we set off, knowing, of course, that he was glad because all he wanted was to have Alice to himself.

Out in the sunlight, along the banks of the stream beyond the pool, the air was warm and sweet. There was vivid green bracken and the drone of insects. We walked till we reached the place where the stream flowed into the river. Then we walked back.

Harold was throwing pebbles into the pool. Alice, with her back to him, stared at the waterfall.

'Did you see any kingfishers?' we asked.

'There was one. At least, it looked like one. But it flew away before we'd time to look at it. But it was nice, wasn't it, Alice?'

'I dunno,' she said. 'Was it?'

'She's got a stomach ache,' said Harold.

She said she didn't want any tea, and half way through she was sick in the pool and wanted to go home. She said the country was a miserable, cold place and she hated it.

We were glad to pack up and go. They trailed behind. Neither of them mentioned bird-watching again and they stayed in the garden, looking at each other. Alice smoothed oil into her legs and arms and lay in the sun hoping for a tan.

Harold read the paper and bounded off to fetch whatever she wanted.

'They two be rum 'uns, ben't they, Will?' said Granny.

'What be so rum about 'em?' Grandfather said.

'It seems they sets about doing nothing all day. Think they'd want to be off out enjoying their selves, wouldn't you?'

'Not if they be keen on one another.'

'They bent any too old,' Granny ventured.

Grandfather rustled the newspaper.

'When they be keen enough, they be old enough,' he said tartly.

There was David who came from Walworth, brought by Granny's relations. Because he liked animals, and they thought he'd enjoy a day in the country.

'He needs some fresh air in his lungs,' they said. 'He's as thin as a rake!'

He blushed as they said this and jerked his chin about.

Later, while he sat scratching his thin arms and blinking in the sun, we gathered round him, admiring him because he was new and different from anyone we'd ever met.

He told us he was a laboratory assistant and looked after the rabbits.

'Do you like looking after the rabbits in a laboratory?' we asked.

''s all right,' he said without enthusiasm, scratching an ear and jerking his chin about again.

I felt sorry for him because he looked as if he had been kept in a dark place away from the daylight. He was puny, and even as he sat in the sun his soft arms began to turn pink.

'I'd like to live in the country,' he said. 'Town gets on my nerves. Too much row. And you never see no flowers. You never know whether it's spring or not. Not in the lousy hole we live in.'

'You've got the rabbits,' we ventured, consolingly.

'They ain't the same as the ones in the medders,' he said. 'The ones we got at the lab is specimens. Most of 'em ain't got no sense. They just sits chewing grub and waiting for what's coming to 'em.'

I was filled with pity for them and him. His indifference was like a cloud passing over the sun.

When he'd gone I heard Granny talking about him to Aunt Georgie.

'Regular, poor little thing he was. A bundle of nerves,' said Aunt Georgie. 'Thin, undernourished. Looked as if he needed a good dollop of suety pudden to line his ribs.'

After a pause, Granny said:

'Funny sort of job he had, didn't he, George?'

'I dunno, did he, Mum?'

'Well, I thought so. Said he worked in a lavatory. Looking after rabbits.'

9

Just as Grandfather had suddenly noticed that the evenings were beginning to draw out, so he suddenly realized they were drawing in.

'The days be drawing in, Nell. Soon have the long, dark nights with us again,' he said.

But the days were still warm. There were sunshine, flowers with the grasses. The overgrown hedgerows had patches of yellow and brown. There were gold leaves in the elms and the Michaelmas daisies were out.

The starlings began to flock. One autumn, vast flocks settled in the rhododendrons on the far side of the common. Black clouds of them went over every evening, in a rush of wings, heading for their dormitory. There were millions and millions. They dropped into the thickets, rustling through the dark green leaves like scattering stones. For over an hour they kept arriving, more and more, flock after flock after flock.

When they settled they began to chatter, first in a general mutter, a tuning-in, a gradual gathering of voices, and then off they went, at full strength, twittering and muttering in a greater and greater crescendo till it filled the whole world. During the tuning-in they were unsettled, fluttering, trying out different perches, seeking better positions, pushing, over-balancing and getting lost in the semi-darkness beneath the leaves. All the time, new arrivals dropped down through the foliage.

I stood on the path in the thickets. I felt as if a monster tide of noise and feathers was engulfing me. I was being swallowed into a sea of birds. The roost had been used for a week or more and every twig and branch was coated with lime, etched out in vivid white, as if suspended in the darkness and appearing and disappearing with the constant movement of the birds, creating a strange illusion. After a while the air began to heat up. Sharp bird-vapours pierced me in stabs, seeming to penetrate my clothes and into my skin.

From time to time something disturbed them: the crack of a twig or the arrival of stragglers. They stopped muttering and rose in a huge, hysterical mob, stirring about in the thickets, screaming in protest, then settled and began to sing again. At last they subsided and were peaceful. The muttering died to a smooth, musical murmur and then stopped.

The smell intensified in the darkness. I had a strange sensation of a world packed with birds.

I put out a hand and touched the warm feathery forms. There was no sound of protest. Nothing but a deathly silence and the warmth of their blood.

10

The changes, when they came, seemed sudden, but actually they had been going on all the time, one thing moving into another, one phase growing towards the next, in order, little by little, gradually, normally and naturally. It only *seemed* that things happened overnight.

When we heard that Miss Littlewood had been taken away, it seemed that something really dramatic had happened.

Mother said:

'Miss Littlewood had always been tottering on the brink of being taken away. Don't get yourselves so worked up about the inevitable.'

Miss Littlewood was the little mad woman who lived with her sister in a cottage in the distant woods we could see from our back garden. In winter, when the trees were bare, the cottage was just visible. We'd always had an odd fancy to see her. The very fact that she was mad was interesting and my sisters and I had never seen a mad woman.

Aunt Georgie, who had once called at the cottage, collecting for the Waifs and Strays, had seen her and we asked over and over again for details.

'What was she like?' we asked.

'Like everyone else, poor little thing.'

'But did she actually *look* daft?'

'No more daft than anyone else.'

'Does she ever come out of the house?'

'No.'

'But *you* saw her . . .'

'She looked through the window. I saw her as I was on the doorstep.'

Fit for a Duchess

'What did she *look* like?'

'Oh, a white face. As white as white it was. And yellow hair, like butter really. And she was just as mad as mad . . . but oh, you children, what a lot you want to know. The poor scatty creature can't *help* being like she is. It isn't nice to be so inquisitive.'

The vision of Miss Littlewood with her white, moon-face and butter-yellow hair intrigued me. I longed to see her for myself and form my own conclusions. And the opportunity came: it had always been there, though we hadn't thought of it before.

It was a hard winter and everything was brittle and cold. Twigs crackled underfoot like bits of ice. The hills were blue with cold. There was snow on the ground and the track to the cottage was untrodden and white as cream. It was Christmas and we were going carol-singing at the cottage. We decided to go on singing till she appeared. We couldn't imagine that she wouldn't appear eventually if we went on singing long enough.

On this day the cottage was like a picture on a Christmas card. It had a thatched roof and small windows with a dim, orange light in one, behind a lace curtain. The window-ledge was full of pot plants. Almost as we reached the door, the lace curtain rippled and a white form appeared in the orange glow.

'Miss Littlewood!' we gasped, trembling with excitement. But it was only a white cat, creeping with curiosity among the pots.

Suddenly, another cat leapt out of the snow and rushed for the house. Another streaked from a hedge and there was yet another in the dead garden growth. The place seemed alive with cats.

We arranged ourselves in a semicircle at the door and began 'While Shepherds Watched' and then, even before we were half way through the first verse, the door was opened by a fragile woman with untidy hair and long skirts. The white cat shot past her and headed for the snow. She smiled and gave us money and then closed the door and the opportunity to see the mad Miss Littlewood seemed to be over.

We felt guilty about the money because we hadn't been singing for it. We knew the sisters were incredibly poor.

'We ought to sing another verse,' we said, and as we began, a white face appeared at the window, a white face surrounded by yellow hair, a face more sad and vague than any we had ever imagined. A pair of white hands came up and fluttered like wings beside it. She laughed and the sound of her laughter was as sweet and sad as the cry of a sea-bird. It was the sound of winter, the cold call of the snow with the echoes of frost in the valleys.

Then she withdrew and suddenly the cold began to sting our ears. The snow began to grow whiter in the dusk and there were no more shadows. We laid the money on the window-sill and rushed away down the long track, half listening as we ran, but there was nothing to hear but the soft fall of the snow among the bare branches overhead.

And in the following spring, she was taken away and the cottage was sold. The news brought a sense of full-stop to what should have been enduring.

And that same spring Grandfather bought some weed-killer for the garden.

'Regular good stuff it is, Nell,' he said. 'All you do is spray it on. It'll kill anything.'

'I dunno as I likes they weedkillers,' said Granny doubtfully.

'They be all right,' said Grandfather. 'It says so on the bottle. It says as it's harmless. Bless us, Nell, you could spray it on your grub and it wouldn't hurt you.'

She sniffed. She made no comment and Grandfather unscrewed the cap and cautiously sniffed the contents.

In those first marvellous days of miracle sprays and

weedkillers, no one saw harm in getting rid of pests so easily, or swiftly abolishing weeds. No one paused to think that the green leaf of the weed was the food for the caterpillar that fed the bird . . .

And suddenly we realized there were no nightingales. The big sandpit in the lane was deserted. The warm spring nights were silent. They'd vanished from the thickets near the crossroads, too, which was extraordinary because it seemed nightingales had been there since the beginning of time.

Many of the cuckoos vanished. Their ceaseless spring chorus dwindled to a few isolated calls like lost echoes in the tops of distant trees.

The lapwings and the snipe were no longer on the common and the curlews had gone.

The linnets, meadow pipits and yellow buntings thinned out.

People said it was the sprays: the building going on; the new roads; the traffic.

The otters had gone from the stream below the waterfall.

'What else can you expect?' said Mother. 'People will hunt and shoot the poor things. They don't stand a chance.'

We heard of a man who had been strolling along the river bank with his gun.

He saw three otters, swimming, line astern with the current, and the only thing he knew about otters was that their skins were money.

'So I took aim at the middle one, hoping I might get all three with luck . . . but I only got the one. And then, of course, I couldn't get the bloody thing out of the water. The others started swimming round it and worked it up onto a sandbank and sat there licking it, making a regular fuss of it. So I left them to it. In any case, it was too shot about to be worth anything . . .'

·　　·　　·　　·　　·

'And nothing tastes like it used to,' said Aunt Rome, one of Mother's friends. 'Haven't you noticed that nothing tastes quite like it used to?'

I remembered the tomatoes Grandfather used to grow under the garden wall. They were small and firm and tasted of the sun and the moss on the stones. You could suck the sweet, cool pips and feel the richness flooding your tongue.

None we bought now tasted like those. The new ones were bigger and redder, like the pictures in the seed catalogues, but tasted bitter and cold. Their juice had a sting that did not come from the sun.

'I don't suppose you young people remember how it was in the countryside,' she went on, talking to my sisters and me. 'I don't suppose you remember all the butterflies and birds. There's nothing like so many now, and unless they start thinking differently, there soon won't be any at all!'

The changes, Aunt Rome was convinced, were caused by the chemical sprays.

The old roadman who worked in our lane said it was the food. There wasn't any nourishment in it any more.

'Take the bacon,' he said. 'You puts it in the pan and it shrivels up to nothink! All you're left with is the bloody pig's squeak and where's the nourishment in a bloody pig's squeak, I'd like to know.'

Some blamed the weather. Some blamed the young. Mother said:

'There's nothing wrong with the young . . . they always get the blame. They're different, that's all. They always have been and they always will be. There'd be something seriously wrong if they weren't.'

Father sucked his teeth and quoted Grandfather:

'As my old father always said: "There always was a seed time and a harvest . . ."'

I went to the waterfall. I wanted to see it because the

trees had been cut, ruining it, some said. Others thought
it was better with the sun getting in and warming the air.

I was open minded. I just wanted to sit by the water
and smell the mud and the fine spray and watch the lacy
green of the beeches, perhaps see a kingfisher, if there
were any left.

But even before I reached the pool, I knew something
had happened.

The hiss of the waterfall filled the valley as it had always
done. The same murmurs were in the stream. The breeze
sounded through the hangers and the evergreens swayed
softly beyond the boathouse. Everything seemed normal
and I reached the edge of the lake and knew it was not.

A glint of silver came from beneath a bramble. There
were unfamiliar, pale grey shapes in the bracken, silver
ones in the dry leaves. All dead fish. And there were dead
fish lying wherever I looked.

I walked on, puzzled. I picked one up. It lay limp, the
dullness of death in its eyes. There were pink glints
around its gills, which lay sucked in. I put it down and
took up another. Then another. I went to the edge of the
water and looked across to the thick reed bed haunted by
ducks and moorhens. A heron flapped out of the bog on
the far side and mounted slowly over the trees and out of
sight.

I talked about the dead fish when I got home. My father
was sitting by the fire, his feet against the brickwork. I
thought he was asleep, but he heard.

'Dynamite!' he said. 'That's what's done that. Too
bloody lazy they are to fish with a line nowadays . . .'

In the big valley on the common, where the pinewoods
were damp and blurred with mist, I saw him kneeling
by a mound of earth.

'Hi, gal,' he said, 'come on over and have a look at
what I got!'

He was the gamekeeper and had been digging out a fox earth. I did not want to look, but he called again.

'Ever seen a fox cub what's bin gassed? I got five of 'em in here. I just bin digging 'em out to make sure they're dead, like.'

He knelt and pushed his arm into the hole and pulled out a small grey animal. It had a strange, grinning expression. Its lips were drawn back in a snarl and its mouth was filled with sand.

'I done 'em in yesterday,' he said, 'all five of the little buggers. Got 'em just right, the old mother and all.'

He pulled another dead cub from the earth and flung it to the ground. It lay like a small cat, with its brush spread in the bracken.

'I gassed another lot over in the wood, night before last, and I got an idea where there's some more. I'll have that lot if I can.'

I had no courage to say what I thought. I stood looking at the dead cubs on the sand and wanted to warm them back to life.

'The little buggers,' he said and took one by its hind leg and flung it aside.

Gradually, the village privies began to vanish. People were doing away with the old bucket system and had nice, indoor conveniences instead.

Father said it wouldn't be long before there wasn't a privy left in the district, except ours. Even that would go eventually. He'd been thinking what could be done to make things better for us. He'd had enough of emptying buckets.

'Troves have done away with their old buckets,' he told us, 'and about time, too. They've been emptying them in twelve square foot of garden for the last fifty years. But in a twelvemonth, they started to dig up what they'd buried the year before. No time for it to rot down.

It isn't good enough. But what else can the poor sods do? They haven't got anywhere else to put it.'

I was walking in the woods at the back of what had once been Miss Littlewood's cottage. Ploughing down the leafy slopes away from the path I saw privy buckets dumped in the undergrowth. There were five, one of them battered and beginning to flake with rust. There were brambles growing through the holes in its sides, and inside were the remains of a robin's nest.

It must have been there for a long time. The others were newer and one of them looked as if it had only just been dumped.

'So *that*'s what people do with them,' I thought, and I wondered what we'd do with ours when the time for it to go arrived.

But our problem was that we were without mains water, and as far as we could see there wasn't much chance of getting it. Then, with unexpected ingenuity, Father decided to make use of the rainwater.

'We get enough of it, in all conscience,' he said. 'We might as well take advantage of it.'

My prayers were about to be answered. There was a prospect of comfort and an easy life. Father said:

'This time we're going to have a really smashing set-up. No string-and-tie-company for us!'

As usual, I had wished for the moon. The porcelain palace I had visualized did not materialize.

The whole system was constructed from bits and pieces left over from other people's jobs. The pipes were an assortment, galvanized ones, iron ones, copper ones.

'They're all right for us,' said Father over and over again as he screwed two odd bits into place.

He dug a huge storage tank at the back of the house connected to all the gutters from the roof.

Into it went the rainwater and everything else that collects on roofs. Down into the tank went the moss and the bird-droppings, the dead beetles and the leaves.

Despite filters, and the various other attempts at purification, grit worked continually into the valves. They seized up, leaked, hissed and refused to work.

This was liable to happen at any time and visitors who were subjected to one of these seizures were puzzled and sometimes alarmed.

They tugged at the chain and emerged worried because they felt they'd broken something.

'It just won't *work* . . .' they said.

'It's the grit,' said Father. 'You have to get up and give the ball-cock a swipe.'

'Go and give the ball-cock a knock will you, dear?' asked Mother smoothly.

I thought it was worse than conducting people up the garden path.

Unpredictable as the system was, it was better than nothing. We looked happily at the rain and knew our new civilization was secure. If the rainfall dwindled we had to be careful, rationing the supply, being co-operative and organizing our private lives as best we could. Drought, of course, finished us.

But even with the water system working smoothly it was incredibly noisy. The cisterns went on hissing loudly all day. There were intestinal rumbles in the tanks and the pipes rapped and created sounds unlike any we had ever heard. Father said it was rust forming inside them.

Every other week, something happened to the taps. They refused to flow, or they flowed and refused to stop. They dripped and the washers wore out. But Father was good at plumbing. He always knew exactly what was wrong. He headed for the most likely valve and blew into it. Or tapped a piece of pipe and announced:

'That's the bugger!'

'Go and turn the stop cock off, gal,' he said to whoever was available.

This meant struggling up through a narrow trapdoor in the bathroom ceiling. It meant climbing onto the edge of the bath and scaling the shelves of the linen cupboard to reach a position in which it was possible to lift oneself through the cavity.

The stop cock, of course, was always jammed.

'It's stuck!' we screamed through the roof into the house below.

'Rusted up, I expect,' said Father. 'Give it a swipe. That'll shift it!' A hammer came hurtling up.

The blows vibrated through the house, shuddering down the pipes to the kitchen taps.

'What on earth *are* you doing?' shouted Mother. 'You'll bring the roof down.'

'There's a difference between kissing me and biting my ear off!' shouted Father.

But the stop cock turned and the water ceased to flow.

'Stop up there while I fix this,' Father went on. 'I'll want it on again in a jiffy and there's no sense clambering down and having to go straight back.'

How often my sisters and I sat up in the dark, windy roof, wondering why stop cocks couldn't be put in more convenient places.

The air was cold and smelt of dry wood. Sour draughts breathed through the tiles and the cobwebs swayed.

After the first minutes of darkness, the structure of the roof began to show. Great, ghostly ribs reached up, holding the tiles. The joists swept ahead like rail tracks into a wide dark tunnel. The chimney stack was a huge, black shape in the centre, supporting the whole house.

One day, as I sat there, waiting for the call to turn the knob, I noticed the relics that had been stored on the platform beside the tank. Picture frames, a print of Captain Scott's Last Journey, old vases, lamps and the zither we had in the bedroom museum.

I lifted it from the dust and plucked a string. With a

groan, it broke, the sound dying as it flung itself away and hung in a limp spiral over the side of the instrument. When I tapped the wood gently with my finger tips, the body of the instrument began to disintegrate, falling into crumbs of decay without even an echo of the music in its strings.

'You all right, gal?' Father called suddenly. 'Not putting your feet between they joists, are you?'

'As if I would!' I thought.

Whenever we went into the roof he gave the same warning about not treading on the laths between the joists: 'Or we'll have the bloody bedroom ceiling down before we know where we are . . .'

These warnings reduced my confidence. I perched, aching and stiff, on the edge of the platform by the tank and listened to the noise of the work downstairs. The echo penetrated into the black corners beyond the chimney and bits of brick fell like rain in the dark, invisible places.

Father always forgot something. A spanner, or a washer, or a special bit of piping. This meant a trip to the workshop where he stopped to talk to one of the men, to discuss the work and ask what else could be done . . . then there'd be a change of plan, new suggestions and finally an exchange of local news. And all the time there I sat, like a cramped owl in the semi-darkness.

It seemed hours later when he called:

'You still up there, gal?'

'Yes and can I come down yet?'

'Yes. Come on down as quick as you can and hold this bloody pipe. If somebody doesn't soon hold it so I can cut it, we'll be mucking about like this till Christmas . . .

'And watch out it doesn't spring back and cut you in two . . .' he said, as I gripped the icy metal in both hands and held on with all my strength.

One day he broke the bakelite seat.

'I knew I'd go and do that sooner or later. The blasted thing wasn't made to stand on. And I can't see what I'm at unless I get up and stick my head in the cistern.'

'Why you don't stand on a chair *I* don't know,' said Mother.

'Because all the chairs in the place are stacked to the ceiling with junk. That's why. And I haven't the time to mess about shifting half the house before I fix a bloody washer.'

It was ages before there was a new seat and in the interim he warned people about the crack.

'Else you'll pinch yer arse,' he added.

Oh yes, it was all rather a let-down. I couldn't help thinking of all the promises about what we would have when the water was laid on—the conveniences upstairs, the everlasting hot water . . .

'But it'll be all right when we're on the mains,' said Father. 'One day we'll be on the mains and there won't be any trouble then.'

That time seemed as remote as Mother's ship.

In the meantime Father was satisfied.

'There's no more buckets to empty,' he said. 'No more pits to dig. We're about as civilized as we've ever been. We've never been so well off.'

I suppose he was right.